Quick Meals from The Curry House

Quick Meals

from

The Curry House

a recipe book by

David Smith

author of

The Curry House

www.curryhouse.co.uk

Contents

Introduction   9

Cooking Notes   13

Ingredients   17

Kitchen Equipment   25

House Specials   29

    Tamarind Chicken   31

    Shahi Chicken   34

    Rezala   37

    Achar   40

    Jeera Murgh   43

    Butter Chicken   46

    Balti   49

    Garlic Chicken   52

    Chicken with Tomatoes and Coriander   55

    Satkara   58

    Pudina Murgh   61

    Chicken Shashlik Bhuna   63

    Chicken with Coconut   66

    Subzi Murgh   69

King Prawn Sizzler   72
Lamb Koftas   75

Curry House Favourites   79

Rogan Josh   81
Bhuna   84
Korma   87
Madras   89
Pasanda   92
Dopiaza   95
Jalfrezi   98
Tikka Masala   101
Saag   104
Dhansak   107
Patia   111
Vindaloo   114

Tandoori-style Dishes   117

Chicken Tikka   119
Tamarind Chicken Tikka   121
Herb Chicken Tikka   123
Tandoori-style Chicken   125
Lamb Chops with Ginger   128
Karahi King Prawns   130
Seekh Kebabs   133

Vegetable Bhajis   135

Oven-Baked Onion Bhajis   137
Bombay Aloo   140
Cauliflower Bhaji   143
Bhindi Bhaji   145
Tarka Dhal   147
Brinjal Bhaji   150
Mushroom Bhaji   153
Saag Bhaji   155
Aloo Gobi (Vegetable Curry)   157

Rice and Bread   161

Pilau Rice   163

Plain Rice   166

griddled Naan   167

Paratha   171

Chapati   174

Dips and Relishes   177

Yoghurt Dip   178

Tamarind Dip   179

Onion Relish   180

Tomato Relish   181

Alternatives to Chicken   183

Lamb   184

King Prawns   186

Vegetarian   188

Substitute Ingredients   191

Notes for American Readers   195

Ingredients and cooking terms   196

Conversion table for weights and measures   198

Online Pictures of the Recipes   201

Index   203

Introduction

All the House Specials and Curry House Favourites in this book can be made from scratch in under an hour. Obviously, if you are making a full meal with vegetable accompaniments and bread you will need longer to get everything ready but it's perfectly easy to make a main dish with rice in under an hour.

Even the recipes that require more that an hour from start to finish do not take up anywhere near that much of your time. The tandoori-style dishes need time for the meat to marinate and the breads need time for the dough to rise or rest. But in all those recipes the actual hands-on time from you the cook is much shorter.

This book is written for people who want to make a restaurant-style meal in a sensible amount of time. For that reason I've left out recipes for starters and desserts because the whole meal would take much longer to prepare. If you want a starter, naan bread and dessert but still want to keep your input to under an hour then the simple solution is to buy everything else from the supermarket. Samosas and onions bhajis can be bought and re-heated in the oven, naan bread can be warmed under the grill and the kulfi for dessert comes straight out of your freezer.

Despite there being no recipes for starters, I have included a recipe for Onion Bhajis. They are so popular I just couldn't leave them out. Besides, many people (including me) like them as part of the main meal rather than as a starter. Instead of deep frying the bhajis like they do in restaurants my recipe bakes them in the oven so they are much easier to cook. There are recipes for naan, parathas and chapatis because they are quite straightforward to make but I have not produced recipes for fancy breads like stuffed parathas and Peshawari naan because the preparation time is far too long.

To keep within my one hour cooking time, I have not included recipes for the more time-consuming dishes from the restaurant menu either. So, for example, there is no recipe for biryani. I do like a good biryani but a **good** biryani can't be made in under an hour. Restaurants can make their biryanis so quickly because they have everything pre-cooked and pre-prepared but that, of course, takes time earlier in the day.

In order to keep things as simple as possible, most of the House Specials and all the Curry House Favourites are written to be made with chicken, but any of the chicken recipes can be made very easily with lamb, king prawns or a vegetarian option instead. All you need to do is amend the recipe using the instructions in the chapter on Alternatives to Chicken.

So, do the recipes come out just like the dishes you get in Indian restaurants? No. The curries fall somewhere between restaurant curries and British supermarket ready-meal curries, although they come out far nearer to restaurant curries than supermarket ones. My recipes for vegetable bhajis are different from restaurant ones too. Many of the vegetable bhajis you find in restaurants are really vegetable curries with lots of oily sauce. Proper bhajis only have a coating sauce, which really brings out the taste of the vegetables, and that's what you'll find in my recipes.

My previous book, The Curry House Cookery Book, shows you how to make restaurant-style curries and other restaurant favourites at home. I designed the recipes so they could be made in a domestic kitchen and, although they are not precise copies of their restaurant equivalents, I had to use a number of restaurant techniques in order to give the recipes that authentic restaurant taste. The disadvantage of using this method is that the recipes take quite a long time to make. A curry base sauce has to be made in advance and the meat and rice have to be pre-cooked. All the recipes in this book are freshly made using individual ingredients. Nothing is pre-prepared.

The recipes are simple and quick to make but they are still restaurant-style dishes rather than home-style dishes of the kind you would find in Indian, Bangladeshi or Pakistani households. Which raises the question, why would you not want home-style meals? Well, home-style meals are quite different from the restaurant meals that most of us non-Asians are used to. We are used to curries with plenty of thick, onion-based sauce. Home-style curries tend to have thinner sauces and often use meat and fish on the bone.

I make no apologies for using the same form of words in the method for all the Curry House Favourites and the House Specials. I should explain that it's not me being lazy or lacking the imagination to write a different form of words for each recipe. Because there is no separate basic curry sauce to make in advance, the puréed onion, garlic and ginger foundation for the curries is made in exactly the same way for each recipe. Once you've made the recipes a few times you'll realise how easy they are to make as the underlying method is always the same. Another advantage of using the same format for all the recipes is that you can easily convert each of the chicken curries into a lamb curry or a prawn curry or a vegetarian curry by following the separate instructions.

The recipes were created or, if they appeared previously in The Curry House Cookery Book, completely revised over a period of two years. I have made all the recipes several times and, in some cases, dozens of times for myself and my family. I then wrote up the recipes from my cooking notes and finally made all the dishes from the finished recipes. So I hope the recipes are straightforward to make and that the dishes turn out for you just like they did for me.

I have thoroughly enjoyed writing this book and am very pleased with all the recipes. I hope you enjoy them too.

David Smith
April 2012

Cooking Notes

portions

All the recipes are designed for two people. If you want to make any of the recipes for four people then simply double the ingredients. For all the Favourite Curries and many of the House Specials you will need to increase the size of the saucepan from the recommended 20cm to at least 24cm to avoid overcrowding the pan. Other than that, doubling the ingredients in the recipes is fine. The one caveat I should add is that the recipes should not be more than doubled. The recipes are not designed for large numbers and you will end up with a curried stew rather than a restaurant-style curry.

simmering

All the curry recipes tell you to simmer the sauce. Simmering is when any liquid in the pan is only <u>just</u> bubbling but not to the point where the sauce is boiling vigorously. Boiling the liquid will ruin the sauce and make the chicken quite tough. Where the recipe says "simmer the chicken for 15 minutes" that means set the timer once the liquid in the curry has started to simmer again and not from the time you put the chicken in the pan.

mashing the onions, garlic and ginger

Take an ordinary, hand-held potato masher and thoroughly mash the onion, garlic and ginger until you get a fairly smooth purée. It doesn't have to look like it's been in a blender, a few odd pieces of onion won't matter. In fact, you'll get a mixture of puréed onions, small bits and larger bits – that's absolutely fine. As the recipes are quick to make, the last thing we want is a messy blender to clean out afterwards and wasting loads of your onion mixture at the same time.

why add water to the curries only 15ml at a time?

If you add all the water at the beginning of the cooking you will end up with a curried stew rather than a restaurant-style curry. Once all the water is in, you won't be able to reduce the liquid without boiling it vigorously, which will ruin the sauce and make the chicken tough.

dry roasting spices and nuts

Dry roasting is an excellent way to intensify the flavour of whole spices or nuts. It is very simple. Take a heavy, dry frying pan and place over a medium heat. Add the spices and stir regularly while the spices heat up. Do not have the heat too high or the spices will burn. The dry-roasting process is finished when you get a warm aromatic smell coming off the spices. Slide the spices onto a plate to cool. For nuts, follow the same process except take the nuts off the heat when they have brown patches all over the surface.

measuring spoons

Apart from very small quantities of spices, which are measured in "pinches" (see below), all spices and most other ingredients in this book are measured by volume. The quantities in the recipes can be achieved by using a set of metric measuring spoons of 2.5ml, 5ml, 10ml and 15ml capacity. So, for example, if the recipe calls for 45ml of vegetable oil then you would use 3 x15ml spoonfuls.

pinch

It is difficult to measure very small amounts of spices. A "pinch" is the amount you can hold between your thumb and index finger. If you're worried about the exact amount then you can try the following experiment – 20 pinches of regular cooking salt should fill a 2.5ml measuring spoon. If you get more or less than 2.5ml from your 20 pinches of salt then adjust the size of one pinch down or up accordingly.

grinds

I have used the term "grinds" as the measurement for black peppercorns. One grind is a quarter turn of a good-sized kitchen pepper mill - not a small table pepper mill.

using ghee in the sauce instead of water

If you like your curries very rich you can add 10ml ghee (clarified butter) or vegetable oil to loosen the curry instead of 10ml water, but that does mean you might get some oil floating on the top of the curry, just as you do in some restaurants. You should only add extra oil to curries where there is a minimum of 200g onions puréed in the sauce and where there is no yoghurt, cream or butter in the recipe. Otherwise the curry will be far too greasy.

kneading dough

Some people think kneading bread dough is a great chore but I enjoy it. I used to go at it hammer and tongs, almost as if kneading bread was an aerobics exercise. All that changed when I read a wonderful book by Dan Lepard called *The Handmade Loaf*. He recommends kneading the dough gently for short periods of time, letting it rest for a while and then kneading it some more. So that's what I do now and it produces far better bread with a lot less effort.

If you've never kneaded bread dough before here's what I do (although I expect Dan Lepard does it quite differently). Take the mound of dough you've just mixed and place it on a large board or clean work surface which has been lightly dusted with flour. Anchor the dough with the ball of your left hand and use the ball of your right hand to push the dough away from you so you're stretching it. Now anchor the dough with the ball of your right hand and stretch the dough with the ball of your left hand. Rotate the dough one quarter turn and, while you are doing so, shape it back into a mound. Repeat the process again and again. Once you've got the hang of it, the stretching and turning becomes rhythmical and you stop thinking consciously about what you need to do next. During the kneading process take a break from time to time and go off to do something else for a few minutes while the dough rests. That's it, and very therapeutic it is too.

re-heating rice

If you have any plain or pilau rice left over you need to be very careful if you are going to keep it for another meal. Rice can host some very nasty bacteria which can survive cooking. If the rice is then kept at room temperature for more than a short time the bacteria can start to multiply and leave behind toxins which cannot be eliminated by subsequent re-heating even at the highest temperatures. The advice from the NHS is as follows:

- cool the rice as quickly as possible (ideally within one hour)
- keep rice in the fridge for no more than one day until reheating
- when you reheat any rice, always check that the dish is steaming hot all the way through
- do not reheat rice more than once

I would strongly advise against ever re-heating rice you bought from a take-away as the rice is likely to have already been re-heated once.

Ingredients

cardamom, ground

You can buy ready-ground cardamom seeds but the powder loses its aroma quite quickly. It is far better and not at all difficult to grind your own cardamom seeds as you need them. Split open a green cardamom pod and take out the little black seeds. Now grind the seeds as best you can in a pestle and mortar. The seeds should easily be crushed under pressure from the pestle. If they just flatten then they are too old and should be thrown away. Use a fresher cardamom pod instead. The grains may end up quite uneven in size but that's OK. If the recipe calls for 3 pinches then use the ground seeds from 1 whole green cardamom pod. If the recipe calls for only 1 or 2 pinches then you will have some left over for another dish.

cassia bark

I have given the approximate length of the pieces of cassia bark to use in the recipes. Being a natural product, cassia bark comes in all sorts of widths. Use pieces, or split wider pieces, that are about 8mm wide.

chicken

Do not overcook chicken or it will end up tough and chewy. On the other hand the chicken must be fully cooked before you serve. Make sure the chicken has turned white all the way through and there is absolutely no pink meat left in the centre.

Never, ever use frozen chicken that is still frozen when you start cooking. Chicken cooked straight from frozen will end up being unbearably tough and you also run the risk of the chicken not being cooked all the way through. So always defrost chicken completely **before** you start cooking. The safest way is to take the chicken out the freezer and place it in the fridge overnight. That way there is no risk of the outer edges of the chicken getting up to room temperature, which is the point when bacteria can begin to multiply.

The recipes say to cut the chicken breasts into chunks 25mm square but this is just an indication of the size you're after. Some pieces will be, for instance, 20mm x 30mm.

chicken mini-fillets

Chicken mini-fillets are commonly sold in packs in British supermarkets. They are ideal for chicken tikka when it is made in a domestic oven. The fillets are small enough to look attractive and brown nicely at the edges but large enough not to dry out while cooking. If you are not familiar with mini-fillets then you can see what I'm talking about by inspecting a regular boned chicken breast. At one edge of the chicken breast there is a long tapering section which can almost be pulled away from the main breast meat. That is the mini-fillet. If you can't buy a pack of mini-fillets then simply take a whole boned chicken breast, cut off the one mini-fillet you do have and then slice the main part of the breast into similar sized pieces. That will work nicely.

chilli powder

Chilli powder is pure ground dried red chillies. Be careful not to buy the sort of chilli powder that is sold to make chili con carne, which is blended with herbs and spices.

All the recipes call for *hot* chilli powder. I used MDH brand Deggi Mirch to test the recipes because it's a hot chilli powder with a consistent heat from pack to pack. It is also a very good-quality product and I can thoroughly recommend it.

The chilli powder measures used in the recipes probably err on the side of caution. You can always increase the heat by adding more chilli powder but once the heat is in you can't take it out. If you like your curries on the hot side then taste the curry about 7 minutes before the end of the cooking and add more chilli powder if you think it's needed. Allow the chilli powder to distribute its heat for a few minutes before you think of adding even more.

You will see from the recipes that the vegetable bhajis use a lot less chilli powder than the curries because there is virtually no sauce to dilute the heat. The grills and tandoori-style dishes are somewhere in between because the heat of the chilli powder is diluted a little by the marinade.

Once you have made a few of the recipes you will know whether my chilli powder measures work for you when using your favourite brand of chilli powder. You can then scale them up or down to suit your own taste.

Supermarket curries are generally not as hot as their restaurant equivalents. The heat in my recipes is typically the strength you'd find in restaurant dishes. So if you want the level of heat you get from a supermarket ready meal then you may need to reduce the chilli powder in the recipes a little.

coconut

Some of the recipes use coconut milk and others use creamed coconut. So what's the difference? The recipe for Chicken with Coconut uses coconut milk instead of water to loosen the sauce. Coconut milk comes in a tin and has a consistency more like single cream than milk. It adds liquid to the sauce and gives it a rich, silky texture as well as the characteristic coconut flavour. Other recipes use creamed coconut, which comes as a solid block. Creamed coconut thickens the sauce as it melts and contains small shreds of coconut, so you're adding a nutty texture as well as flavour. Some shops also sell "coconut cream" which is sold in small tins and is concentrated coconut milk. It is not as easy to find as either coconut milk or creamed coconut so I have not used it in the recipes although I do use it at home, especially in Thai cooking.

coriander leaves

Quite a few of the recipes call for finely chopped coriander leaves. You can include the fine stalks too but not the coarser ones. Wash the coriander leaves and dry them thoroughly on kitchen paper. Remove the leaves from the coarser stalks and finely chop with the curved blade of a chef's chopping knife (see

Kitchen Equipment). Measure the chopped leaves by sliding them into a measuring spoon and gently tapping the spoon down to make sure it's full. Do not push the chopped leaves down into the measuring spoon so they are tightly packed.

cumin seeds, dry-roasted and ground

All the dips and relishes and some of the other recipes use ground, dry-roasted cumin seeds. Dry roast the cumin seeds (see Cooking Notes) and let them cool. Then grind the seeds using a pestle and mortar. The seeds grind quite easily so it's not a great effort and it's much better to roast and grind a fresh batch each time you cook.

English mint sauce

Some of the recipes use commercially made mint sauce. The best available in the UK is made by Colman's. If you can't get hold of any English mint sauce then you can make a decent substitute yourself. Finely chop some fresh mint leaves and mix in a little bowl with red wine vinegar and some sugar. Adjust the balance of sugar to vinegar so you get a pleasant sweet/sour taste which is neither too acid nor too sweet. Then use the amount stated in the recipe. It is best made well in advance to bring out the full flavour of the mint.

garam masala – where is it?

Surely all Indian dishes use garam masala? Well, yes and no. Firstly, we are not making authentic home-style dishes here; dishes where the spices are all lovingly dry roasted and freshly ground for each dish. We are making restaurant-style dishes using mostly pre-ground spices. Commercially made garam masala is hugely variable in its composition and taste. You could make the same curry with six different brands of garam masala and you would get six different-tasting dishes. Conversely, if you use your favourite shop-bought garam masala (or even your own home-blended masala) for every dish they will all end up tasting uncomfortably similar. To quote from Classic Cooking of Punjab by Jiggs Kalra, Pushpesh Pant and Raminder Malhotra (a scholarly and excellent book published in New Delhi): "It would be absurd to reduce every dish to the lowest common denominator by using the same combination for every dish. The secret of good cooking is to make a separate garam masala for each dish". Now, we don't have the time to do that if we are making each curry in under an hour so my solution is to use different combinations of aromatic and warm (garam) spices for each dish – that is why you will see time and time again in my recipes "add a pinch" of this or "add 2 pinches" of that.

garlic

Use decent-sized cloves of garlic and avoid those skinny little ones. Trim the garlic and remove the papery outer skin. It's handy to leave the root end on the garlic and use it as a "handle" to hold while you grate the garlic. Throw the end away afterwards. Watch out for garlic which has been stored for too long. The cloves will feel very light for their size and they really are past their best. That's the time to buy a new bulb of garlic.

ghee

Ghee is clarified butter and can be used for frying instead of vegetable oil. Unlike vegetable oil, ghee is high in saturated fats. Ghee can be used instead of water to loosen the sauce in some curries – see Cooking Notes.

ginger

Peel the ginger and grate it using a fine-bladed, hand-held grater. The recipes measure grated ginger by volume usually relative to the volume of grated garlic. Ginger root (actually not a root but a rhizome) comes in all shapes and sizes, so to say "use 2cm of ginger" like some recipes do is far too imprecise.

lemon/lime juice

The recipes all use freshly squeezed juice from ripe lemons or limes. Do not use preserved juice as it will not have the required fresh taste.

mint leaves

Wash the fresh mint leaves and cut the leaves off the stalk. Finely chop the leaves with the curved blade of a chef's chopping knife. Measure the chopped leaves by sliding them into a measuring spoon and gently tapping the spoon down to make sure it's full. Do not push the chopped leaves down into the measuring spoon so they are tightly packed.

onion

It's easy to describe the size of onions as small, medium or large but, as each person's perception can vary so much, it's not very helpful. So in the recipes you will find that I have stated the trimmed weight of onion to be used. The trimmed weight is the weight after removing the growing tip, the root end, the papery skin and maybe the outer layer of the onion if it has brown patches on it. There are some recipes that do call for an additional "half a medium onion" to fry in strips and add to the curry. In those instances, the precise weight isn't so important but a rule of thumb would be to use about 75g.

salt

The amount of salt you add to the recipes is really a matter of taste. You certainly won't need the excessive amounts used in some restaurants. As a rough guide, I use just under half a 2.5ml spoon of salt in the curries. Use less in the stir-fries, vegetable bhajis and tandoori-style dishes. Be careful when adding salt to dishes which include tamarind paste, which already contains a fair amount of salt. You will need to reduce your regular amount of salt accordingly. The same goes for the Achar recipe as the lime pickle used also tends to be fairly salty.

tamarind paste

Tamarind paste has a consistency similar to tomato ketchup. It is not thick and sticky like tamarind concentrate and not wet and sloppy like tamarind juice. If you live in the UK, Barts Spices sell an excellent tamarind paste in 100g jars. It has the best taste of all the manufactured tamarind products.

tomato

A "good-sized" tomato weighs roughly 100g before preparation. Always use ripe tomatoes and try not to use ones that wouldn't be ripe enough to eat raw. If you have to use slightly unripe tomatoes you may find you need to add a pinch or two of sugar to the sauce to avoid it being too sour.

tomato paste

What the rest of the world calls tomato paste, we in the UK confusingly call tomato purée; if you look carefully at the description on the tube or tin you will see that it is actually labelled as "double-concentrated tomato purée". I have used the term tomato paste in the recipes as it is a more accurate description. Tomato purée is wet and sloppy while tomato paste is, well, a thick paste sold in tubes or small cans.

yoghurt – Greek-style full fat

Greek-style yoghurt has a fat content of about 10%. The high fat content ensures that the yoghurt will not easily split into solids and liquids when heated. Do not substitute low-fat or fat-free yoghurt for the full-fat yoghurt in the recipes.

Kitchen Equipment

The main pieces of kitchen equipment you need to make the recipes are listed here. All the items are easily available from any good cook shop, except maybe the karahi. If you don't own a karahi then use a large wok instead.

hand-held food grater

You don't need anything fancy to grate your garlic and ginger. All that's needed is an ordinary hand-held metal food grater with fine textured cutters. Do make sure to scrape all the ginger and garlic off the back of the grater so you don't waste any.

heavy-bottomed casserole pan - 20cm diameter

I use a cast-iron Le Creuset casserole pan to make my curries. They are horribly expensive but they will last you a lifetime. If your budget doesn't stretch to a Le Creuset pan then any pan with a thick, heavy base will do. If your pan doesn't have a solid-enough base your sauces will tend to catch and burn on the bottom of the pan. The heavy base conducts heat evenly so you can use a very low heat to simmer the sauce. Don't use a pan smaller than 20cm in diameter or you will overcrowd it. If you want to double the amount of the curry recipes you will need to use a larger 24cm pan.

potato masher

A cheap, hand-held potato masher is all you need to give your curries a sauce with the right texture. An electric blender is not necessary to purée the onion, garlic and ginger foundation for the sauce. By using a potato masher instead of a blender you'll get a mixture of puréed onions, small bits and larger bits, which is exactly what you want.

metric measuring spoons

The recipes all use metric volume measurements for the spices and liquids. If you're going to follow the recipes accurately you will need some proper measuring spoons with a capacity of 2.5ml, 5ml, 10ml and 15ml.

pestle and mortar

All you need for grinding cardamom seeds or dry-roasted cumin seeds is a pestle and mortar. The recipes use only small amounts of ground seeds so there's no need to grind large batches in an electric grinder.

cook's chopping knife

You need a broad-bladed knife with a curved cutting edge to finely chop anything. This type of knife is excellent for chopping herbs like coriander and mint. Rocking the knife over and over again on the leaves will give you finely chopped herbs.

small-capacity kitchen scales

It is very useful to have scales that will measure small amounts accurately. If you try and measure 50g on kitchen scales that can weigh up to 5 kilos you will find it very difficult to get an accurate measurement. My scales will weigh a maximum of 500g and will measure accurately down to 10g. They are sometimes called "diet scales".

karahi - 31cm diameter

The South Asian karahi is similar in shape to a Chinese wok, although it often has a flat, rather than a rounded, base. The karahi has two small handles on either side rather than one long handle like the wok. This type of bowl-shaped cooking utensil is excellent for stir frying. Because the pan has a large surface area you can toss the ingredients around in oil and quickly fry them rather than having them steam in their own liquid. Use a wok instead if you already have one. The recipes all need a large karahi which should have a diameter of 30 to 31cm.

baking tray and wire rack

If you are going to make the tandoori-style dishes then you are going to need these two cheap but useful pieces of equipment. You may have to buy them separately. The baking tray should be made of the thickest gauge metal possible to stop it buckling in the heat of the oven. It should measure about 35cm by 28cm at the inside edges. The wire rack should have a close mesh – a rack for cooling cakes is ideal. The rack should be just smaller than the baking tray so that the wire feet sit on the bottom of the tray.

cast-iron griddle - 26cm diameter

The recipes for naan, chapatis and paratha all use a cast-iron griddle to cook the bread. Season your griddle according to the instructions that came with it and it will become more non-stick every time you use it. I also use mine to re-heat shop-bought naan, pizzas and tortillas, so it gets a lot of use in my kitchen.

small-capacity food blender

If you are making the recipes for Chicken Tikka Masala or Shahi Chicken which call for cashew nut purée then you will need a small-capacity food blender. A baby food blender is ideal.

House Specials

It would be difficult to find an Indian restaurant these days that didn't offer a selection of house specials or chef's special dishes. Many restaurants present their specials on the menu alongside the standard curry house curries. Some more upmarket restaurants have dropped the familiar curries completely and their menus only offer authentic regional dishes.

Quite a few of the house specials in restaurants are Bangladeshi specialities, which is not too surprising since the majority of "Indian" restaurants in Britain are run by people of Bangladeshi origin. Chef's specials are usually more expensive than the standard curries on the menu because they take longer to prepare and contain extra spices or additional ingredients. Each of my House Specials has its own masala of spices and all the recipes can be made in under an hour.

I have included my version of two Bangladeshi specialities, Rezala and Satkara, in this chapter. Chefs tend to modify traditional recipes to make them suitable for restaurant cooking and I have made my own interpretations of my favourite restaurant versions. So you will not be making authentic dishes from my recipes, although I don't think you'll mind when you taste them.

Balti dishes were popularised in Britain by Birmingham's Pakistani restaurateurs but have since become part of the standard curry menu in regular Indian restaurants. My version takes its inspiration from Birmingham's

Balti House originals. Chicken with Coconut has a South Indian influence and is made with coconut milk and garnished with toasted coconut.

Some of the House Specials are curries flavoured with a key ingredient. Tamarind Chicken is hot, sweet and sour. Pudina Murgh is a big favourite of mine and has a sauce flavoured with fresh mint. Jeera Murgh includes cumin seeds prepared in three different ways. Achar is another hot, sweet-and-sour curry with the sour flavour coming from lime pickle and fresh limes.

Two of the specials have deliciously rich sauces. Butter Chicken, or Murgh Makhani, contains butter, cream and fresh tomato purée. Shahi Chicken is a Moghul-style dish with a smooth sauce thickened with roasted cashew nut purée.

Not all the recipes are curries with an abundance of sauce. Chicken with Tomatoes and Coriander is a fresh-tasting dish with a lovely contrast of flavours. Subzi Murgh is a warmly spiced dish of chicken cooked with onions and other vegetables. Some dishes only have a coating sauce. Garlic Chicken is a stir-fry with courgettes, tomatoes and fresh coriander. King Prawn Sizzler is made with succulent jumbo king prawns stir fried with onions and sweet peppers.

Finally, there are a couple of quite unusual dishes. Chicken Shashlik Bhuna is the speciality of a favourite restaurant of mine and, as the name suggests, is a fusion of two well-known dishes. Lamb Kofta is an authentic dish and is only unusual because it doesn't appear on restaurant menus very often. Kofta are delicious little meatballs which are firstly fried and then cooked in a creamy sauce.

It was great fun creating these recipes and even more enjoyable testing them and tasting them. The specials make a refreshing change from the old curry house favourites and I hope you enjoy trying them.

Tamarind Chicken

Tamarind Chicken is hot, sweet and sour – my perfect combination.

Because you are making it at home you can, of course, make it however hot or mild you like. This recipe comes out medium-hot. You can also change the sweet/sour balance to your own liking by adding more tamarind paste or more sugar.

Tamarind paste has a consistency similar to tomato ketchup. It is not thick and sticky like tamarind concentrate and not wet and sloppy like tamarind juice. If you live in the UK, Barts Spices sell an excellent tamarind paste in 100g jars. It has the best taste of all the manufactured tamarind products. You could buy dried tamarind pods and make the paste yourself but it would take ages to boil the pods, sieve out the seeds, scrape off the pulp from the underside of the sieve and then finally concentrate the tamarind juice into a paste. It is far better to let Barts or some other good company do all the hard work for you.

ingredients

45ml vegetable oil
200g onions – finely chopped
2 cloves garlic – finely grated
grated ginger (about half the
  volume of the garlic)
45ml water

350g chicken breast

5ml ground coriander seed
5ml ground cumin seed
2.5ml **hot** chilli powder
2.5ml turmeric
2.5ml paprika

Heat 45ml oil in the heavy-bottomed pan on a medium heat. While the oil is heating up, finely chop the onion.

When the oil is hot, add the chopped onion to the pan and stir fry for 5 minutes. The onions should not brown, so lower the heat a little if they start to fry too hard.

While the onions are frying, grate the garlic and ginger onto a small plate but make sure to give the onions a good stir from time to time so they don't start browning.

Spoon the grated garlic and ginger into the pan (plus any juices left on the plate). Stir in well and stir fry continuously for 2 minutes.

2 pinches ground cloves

4 pinches ground cardamom
   seeds

30ml tamarind paste

15ml tomato paste

2.5ml sugar

2 grinds of black peppercorns

salt (the tamarind paste is
   likely to be salty so use less
   salt than normal)

water to loosen the sauce

15ml finely chopped coriander
   leaves

more finely chopped coriander
   leaves to garnish

kitchen equipment

hand-held food grater with fine
   holes

potato masher

20cm heavy-bottomed pan

Add 45ml water and mix in thoroughly.

Once the liquid starts to boil put a lid on the pan, turn the heat down to minimum and cook for 20 minutes. Do not remove the lid during this time.

While the onion mixture is cooking, skin the chicken breasts, remove any connective tissue and cut the meat into chunks about 25mm square.

When the onion mixture is cooked, take the pan off the heat and remove the lid. Now take a potato masher and thoroughly mash the onions, garlic and ginger until you get a fairly smooth purée.

Return the pan to the heat, still at its lowest setting, and add the ground coriander, ground cumin, chilli powder, turmeric, paprika, ground cloves and ground cardamom seeds.

Warm through the spices for about 1 minute, stirring all the time.

Raise the heat to medium and add the chicken chunks. Stir until the pieces of chicken have turned white over most of their surface.

Add the tamarind paste, tomato paste, sugar, black pepper, salt and 15ml water. Stir to mix all the ingredients and bring the mixture to a simmer.

Simmer the chicken for 15 minutes (less if you used small chunks).

If the mixture starts getting a little dry add 15ml water – no more just yet. As the chicken is cooking, add more water if the sauce gets too dry but, again, only 15ml at a time.

Towards the end of the cooking taste the curry and adjust the sweet/sour balance if you think it's not quite right by adding a little more tamarind paste or a little more sugar.

2 minutes before the chicken is ready add 15ml finely chopped coriander leaves and stir to mix.

Check that the chicken is thoroughly cooked. Serve garnished with more chopped coriander leaves.

Shahi Chicken

Shahi means royal and this curry lives up to its name. The cashew nut purée gives a delicious nutty flavour, the yoghurt provides a creamy texture and the cardamom gives a very special taste.

When I first made this dish I used an electric spice grinder (really a small coffee grinder that I keep just for spices) to purée the cashews. What I learnt to my cost is that spice grinders need **dry** ingredients. I know cashew nuts look dry but their high oil content means that by the time you've got rid of all the chunks you have a paste that looks and acts like putty and which will clog up the grinding mechanism for ever. Use a small-capacity food blender instead so you can add water to make a purée rather than a paste. Don't reduce the quantity of cashew nut purée that you make. I have done many tests and you need the amounts stated in the recipe to guarantee a smooth purée. You will have some left over but it freezes very well.

If you can't get raw unsalted cashew nuts then buy the ready-salted, dry-roasted kind and wash off the salt in a sieve, or use as they are and reduce the normal amount of salt you'd use in the recipe.

ingredients

30ml vegetable oil

150g onions – finely chopped

25mm piece cassia bark

2 cloves garlic – finely grated

grated ginger (about the same volume as the garlic)

45ml water

350g chicken breast

50g unsalted, raw cashew nuts

5ml ground coriander seed

Heat 30ml oil in the heavy-bottomed pan on a medium heat. While the oil is heating up, finely chop the onion.

When the oil is hot, add the piece of cassia bark, stir to coat it with oil, then add the chopped onion and stir fry for 5 minutes. The onions should not brown, so lower the heat a little if they start to fry too hard.

While the onions are frying, grate the garlic and ginger onto a small plate but make sure to give the onions a good stir from time to time so they don't start browning.

2.5ml ground cumin seed

⅓ of a 2.5ml spoon *hot* chilli powder

⅔ of a 2.5ml spoon turmeric

3 pinches ground cardamom seeds

2 pinches ground mace (or ground nutmeg)

30ml Greek-style full fat yoghurt

2 grinds of black peppercorns

salt to taste (be careful if you used salted cashews)

½ a 2.5ml spoon sugar

10ml butter cut into small chunks

water to loosen the sauce

finely chopped coriander leaves to garnish

kitchen equipment

hand-held food grater with fine holes

potato masher

20cm heavy-bottomed pan

small-capacity food blender – a baby food blender is ideal

rubber spatula

Spoon the grated garlic and ginger into the pan (plus any juices left on the plate). Stir in well and stir fry continuously for 2 minutes.

Add 45ml water and mix in thoroughly.

Once the liquid starts to boil put a lid on the pan, turn the heat down to minimum and cook for 20 minutes. Do not remove the lid during this time.

While the onion mixture is cooking, skin the chicken breasts, remove any connective tissue and cut the meat into chunks roughly 25mm square.

Now make the cashew nut purée. Dry roast 50g cashew nuts on a medium/low heat until they are covered in nice brown patches. Let the roasted cashew nuts cool a little and then place them in a small blender together with 75ml water. Blend well until very smooth. Pour out the cashew nut purée into a small bowl and scrape round the blender with a rubber spatula to get all the remaining purée out of the blender.

When the onion mixture is cooked, take the pan off the heat and remove the lid. Remove the cassia bark and set aside. Now take a potato masher and thoroughly mash the onions, garlic and ginger until you get a fairly smooth purée.

Return the pan to the heat, still at its lowest setting, and add the ground coriander, ground cumin, chilli powder, turmeric, ground cardamom seeds and ground mace.

Warm through the spices for about 1 minute, stirring all the time. Return the cassia bark to the pan.

Raise the heat to medium and add the chicken chunks. Stir until the pieces of chicken have turned white over most of their surface.

Add the yoghurt and stir until the yoghurt has blended with the onion and spice mixture.

Add the black pepper, salt, sugar, 45ml cashew nut purée and 15ml water to the pan.

Stir to mix all the ingredients and bring the mixture to a simmer.

Simmer the chicken for 15 minutes (less if you used small chunks).

If the mixture starts getting a little dry add 15ml water – no more just yet. As the chicken is cooking, add more water if the sauce gets too dry but, again, only 15ml at a time. Make sure the sauce is not too liquid before you add the butter as the butter will loosen the sauce.

1 minute before the chicken is ready add the small chunks of butter and very gently heat through, stirring all the time. Do NOT bring the sauce to a boil or the butter will split.

Check that the chicken is thoroughly cooked. Remove the piece of cassia bark. Serve garnished with finely chopped coriander leaves.

Rezala

Rezala is a Bangladeshi dish which has found its way onto the specials menu of many restaurants in the last 10 years or so. It is usually offered as either Lamb Rezala or Chicken Rezala. I have to say that, for a traditional dish, the recipe seems to vary quite a lot from restaurant to restaurant.

The following recipe is my favourite and is flavoured with aromatic spices, yoghurt and green chillies but it is probably not very authentic. Traditional recipes sometimes add kewra water (made from screw pine flowers) or rose water to the finished dish to give it an added floral aroma. You can if you like but I don't tend to bother.

The number of chillies you use is up to you and will depend on your taste and the heat of the chillies. The end result should be medium/hot. The heat in fresh chillies can be extremely variable so if you want your rezala to be mild you can omit the fresh chillies and replace them with thin strips of green sweet pepper plus a little chilli powder. I don't like the taste of this as much but it's a decent alternative.

ingredients

45ml vegetable oil
1 dried bay leaf
200g onions – finely chopped
2 cloves garlic – finely grated
grated ginger (about the same
   the volume as the garlic)
45ml water

350g chicken breast
4 – 8 thin green chillies

5ml ground coriander seed
2.5ml ground cumin seed
½ a 2.5ml spoon turmeric

Heat 45ml oil in a 20cm, heavy-bottomed pan on a medium heat. While the oil is heating up, finely chop the onion.

When the oil is hot, add the bay leaf and stir so it is coated in oil. Now add the chopped onion to the pan and stir fry for 5 minutes. The onions should not brown so lower the heat a little if they start to fry too hard.

While the onions and bay leaf are frying, grate the garlic and ginger onto a small plate but make sure to give the onions a good stir from time to time so they don't start browning.

Spoon the grated garlic and ginger into the pan (plus any juices left on the plate). Stir in well and stir fry

3 pinches ground cloves

2 pinches ground mace (or nutmeg)

3 pinches ground cardamom seeds

45ml Greek-style full fat yoghurt

2 grinds of black peppercorns

salt

½ a 2.5ml spoon sugar

water to loosen the sauce

some green chillies, sliced diagonally, to garnish

kitchen equipment

hand-held food grater with fine holes

potato masher

20cm heavy-bottomed pan

continuously for 2 minutes.

Add 45ml water and mix in thoroughly.

Once the liquid starts to boil put a lid on the pan, turn the heat down to minimum and cook for 20 minutes. Do not remove the lid during this time.

While the onion mixture is cooking, skin the chicken breasts, remove any connective tissue and cut the meat into chunks about 25mm square.

Slice the stalks off the chillies and cut them in half lengthways. Remove the seeds and pith by sliding a teaspoon along the length of the chilli half. Set aside.

When the onion mixture is cooked, take the pan off the heat and remove the lid. Remove the bay leaf from the pan and set aside. Now take a potato masher and mash the onions, garlic and ginger until you get a fairly smooth purée.

Return the pan to the heat, still at its lowest setting, and add the ground coriander, ground cumin, turmeric, ground cloves, ground mace and ground cardamom seeds.

Warm through the spices for about 1 minute, stirring all the time to mix them in thoroughly. Return the bay leaf to the pan.

Raise the heat to medium and add the chicken chunks. Stir until the pieces of chicken have turned white over most of their surface.

Add 45ml Greek-style yoghurt and stir until the yoghurt has blended with the onion and spice mixture.

Add the black pepper, salt and sugar. Stir to mix all the ingredients and bring the mixture to a simmer.

Simmer the chicken for 15 minutes (less if you used small chunks).

If the mixture starts getting a little dry add 15ml water – you probably won't need any more than that.

10 minutes before the chicken in ready, add the chilli halves and stir to mix. Poke the chilli halves down into the liquid so they cook right through and spread their heat into the sauce.

Check that the chicken is thoroughly cooked. Remove the bay leaf and discard it.

Serve garnished with some fresh chillies that have been sliced diagonally.

Achar

If you are a subscriber to The Curry House Premium Area you may recognise this recipe and the following description. The recipe first appeared in the Premium Area as a bonus recipe. I liked the recipe so much I wanted to include it in this book, so I have converted the recipe to the quick method used for all the other curries in this chapter.

Achar Gosht (lamb) and Achar Murgh (chicken) are becoming very popular chef's specials in many restaurants but there are two distinct versions of this dish. The word achar means "pickle" and the traditional way of cooking Achar Gosht is to use the spices which are usually used in South Asian pickles (namely fennel, kalonji, mustard seed and fenugreek seed) to flavour the dish. The other version, favoured by many restaurants, is to use ready-prepared pickle in the sauce and add the flavour that way. I have followed the restaurant example and used lime pickle.

The one problem with this recipe is that the key flavouring, lime pickle, can vary in composition and taste according to which brand you use. I have had great success using the Rajah brand but Patak's Medium Lime Pickle is more widely available and gives reasonable results.

If you can't get hold of a decent jar of lime pickle then don't worry. Simply substitute the fresh lime combination mentioned in "special notes" below.

ingredients

45ml vegetable oil
2 pinches fennel seeds
2 pinches kalonji
250g onions – finely chopped
2 cloves garlic – finely grated
grated ginger (about half the
   volume of the garlic)
60ml water

Heat 45ml oil in a 20cm, heavy-bottomed pan on a medium heat. While the oil is heating up, finely chop the onion.

When the oil is hot, add the fennel seeds and kalonji and stir so they are coated in oil. Now add the chopped onion to the pan and stir fry for 5 minutes. The onions should not brown, so lower the heat a little if they start to fry too hard.

350g chicken breast

7.5ml ground coriander seed

5ml ground cumin seed

2.5ml *hot* chilli powder for a
medium lime pickle – less for a
hot pickle

2.5ml turmeric

2.5ml paprika

15ml finely chopped medium
lime pickle

2.5ml English mint sauce
(preferably Colman's)

2.5ml lime juice

2.5ml sugar

2 grinds of black peppercorns

salt (but see special notes below)

water to loosen the sauce

[optional] 10ml ghee or
vegetable oil

[optional] more fresh lime juice
or extra sugar to adjust the
sweet/sour balance

twists of lime to garnish

special notes

The lime pickle is likely to be
fairly hot so be careful how
much chilli powder you use.

Add salt sparingly – the lime
pickle will be quite salty.

While the onions and spices are frying, grate the
garlic and ginger onto a small plate but make sure to
give the onions a good stir from time to time so they
don't start browning.

Spoon the grated garlic and ginger into the pan (plus
any juices left on the plate). Stir in well and stir fry
continuously for 2 minutes.

Add 60ml water and mix in thoroughly.

Once the liquid starts to boil put a lid on the pan, turn
the heat down to minimum and cook for 20 minutes.
Do not remove the lid during this time.

While the onion mixture is cooking, skin the chicken
breasts, remove any connective tissue and cut the
meat into chunks about 25mm square.

Prepare the lime pickle. Spoon some of the solid bits
out of the jar, place them on a chopping board and
chop finely. You need enough chopped lime pickle to
fill a 15ml measuring spoon.

Slice a lime in half and cut thin slices from one half
for the garnish. Cut each circular slice once from the
centre to the edge and make a twist. Set aside. Use
the other half of the lime to squeeze some lime juice.

When the onion mixture is cooked, take the pan off
the heat and remove the lid. Now take a potato
masher and thoroughly mash the onions, garlic and
ginger until you get a fairly smooth purée.

Return the pan to the heat, still at its lowest setting,
and add the ground coriander, ground cumin, chilli
powder, turmeric and paprika.

Warm through the spices for about 1 minute, stirring
all the time to mix them in thoroughly.

If you can't get any decent lime pickle then very finely chop ¼ of a whole, fresh lime (use all the skin, pith and juice) and use that plus 2 pinches dried fenugreek leaves and 2 pinches ground cloves instead.

kitchen equipment

hand-held food grater with fine
    holes
potato masher
20cm heavy-bottomed pan

Raise the heat to medium and add the chicken chunks. Stir until the pieces of chicken have turned white over most of their surface.

Add the finely chopped lime pickle, English mint sauce, lime juice, sugar, black pepper, salt and 30ml water. Stir to mix all the ingredients and bring the mixture to a simmer.

Simmer the chicken for 15 minutes (less if you used small chunks).

If the mixture starts getting a little dry add 15ml water – no more just yet. As the chicken is cooking, add more water if the sauce gets too dry but, again, only 15ml at a time. If you like your curries very rich you could add 10ml ghee or vegetable oil to loosen the curry instead of 10ml water.

Towards the end of the cooking taste the curry and adjust the sweet/sour balance if you think it's not quite right by adding a little more lime juice or a little more sugar.

Check that the chicken is thoroughly cooked. Serve garnished with twists of lime.

Jeera Murgh

My recipe for Jeera Murgh uses cumin seeds, *jeera*, in three different forms.

Firstly, whole cumin seeds are dry roasted in a heavy pan and then ground to give a deep, smoky flavour. Then, whole cumin seeds are fried with the onions and left whole to give a nice cumin hit when you bite into one. Finally, regular ground cumin is used in the masala to round out the taste.

There are many different recipes for jeera murgh. Some, like the one in Cyrus Todiwala's book Café Spice Namaste, are dry stir-fries rather than curries. Cyrus's recipe uses small chunks of chicken which are quickly fried with crushed cumin seeds and lemon juice and served as a starter or snack. My recipe is a curry with a thick spicy sauce and is more like the style you'll find on the list of chef's specials on an Indian restaurant menu.

ingredients

45ml vegetable oil
200g onions – finely chopped
3 pinches whole cumin seeds
25mm piece cassia bark
2 cloves garlic – finely grated
grated ginger (about half the
    volume of the garlic)
45ml water

350g chicken breast
5ml whole cumin seeds to dry
    roast

5ml ground coriander seed
5ml ground cumin seed (regular)
2.5ml **hot** chilli powder
2.5ml turmeric
2.5ml paprika

Heat 45ml oil in a 20cm, heavy-bottomed pan on a medium heat. While the oil is heating up, finely chop the onion.

When the oil is hot, add 3 pinches of whole cumin seeds and the cassia bark and stir so they are coated in oil. Now add the chopped onion to the pan and stir fry for 5 minutes. The onions should not brown, so lower the heat a little if they start to fry too hard.

While the onions and spices are frying, grate the garlic and ginger onto a small plate but make sure to give the onions a good stir from time to time so they don't start browning.

Spoon the grated garlic and ginger into the pan (plus any juices left on the plate). Stir in well and stir fry continuously for 2 minutes.

Add 45ml water and mix in thoroughly.

2 pinches ground cloves

30ml Greek-style (full fat)
   yoghurt
2 grinds of black peppercorns
salt to taste
3 pinches sugar

water to loosen the sauce
finely chopped coriander leaves
   to garnish

kitchen equipment

hand-held food grater with fine
   holes
potato masher
20cm heavy-bottomed pan
pestle and mortar
small frying pan

Once the liquid starts to boil put a lid on the pan, turn the heat down to minimum and cook for 20 minutes. Do not remove the lid during this time.

While the onion mixture is cooking, skin the chicken breasts, remove any connective tissue and cut the meat into chunks about 25mm square.

Dry roast 5ml cumin seeds in a small frying pan. Once the seeds start to give off a lovely, warm aroma slide them out of the pan and onto a plate. Let the seeds cool and then grind them as finely as you can with a pestle and mortar. They don't have to be as evenly ground as commercially ground spices, so don't be too particular. You won't use all that you've ground so save what's left over in some cling film for use another day.

When the onion mixture is cooked, take the pan off the heat and remove the lid. Remove the cassia bark and set aside. Now take a potato masher and mash the onions, garlic and ginger until you get a fairly smooth purée.

Return the pan to the heat, still at its lowest setting, and add the ground coriander, regular ground cumin, chilli powder, turmeric, paprika and ground cloves (but not, at this point, the ground dry-roasted cumin seeds you just made).

Warm through the spices for about 1 minute stirring all the time to mix them in thoroughly.

Raise the heat to medium and add the chicken chunks. Stir until the pieces of chicken have turned white over most of their surface. Return the cassia bark to the pan.

Add 30ml Greek-style yoghurt and stir until the yoghurt has blended with the onion and spice mixture. Then add the black pepper, salt and sugar.

Stir to mix all the ingredients and bring the mixture to a simmer. Simmer the chicken for 15 minutes (less if you used small chunks).

If the mixture starts getting a little dry add 15ml water – no more just yet. As the chicken is cooking, add more water if the sauce gets too dry but, again, only 15ml at a time.

7 minutes before the end of the cooking add 2.5ml of your ground, dry roasted cumin seeds. Stir to mix.

Remove the cassia bark. Check that the chicken is thoroughly cooked. Serve garnished with finely chopped coriander leaves.

Butter Chicken

Butter Chicken, or Murgh Makhani, is a classic Indian dish.

Traditionally Murgh Makhani is made with tandoori chicken but that would make this recipe too time consuming, so we'll use plain chicken instead. The recipe includes the three classic ingredients for the makhani sauce: butter, cream and puréed tomatoes.

I really enjoy making this recipe; the ingredients just seem to be made for each other. The tartness of the tomatoes is offset by the butter and the cream. The dish is lightly spiced but full of flavour. Of all the mild curries this is my absolute favourite. It is a bit heavy on saturated fat from the butter and the cream but it does redeem itself when you taste it. This is **the** classic creamy curry.

There's no need for artificial food colouring in this dish. It has a beautiful warm orange colour all of its own. If you search Google images for "butter chicken" you'll see that many come out a deep red colour courtesy of food colouring (believe me, you don't get that deep red colour from tomato paste or paprika or anything natural) . To my mind that's OK for Chicken Tikka Masala because it's a restaurant invention but, for a traditional dish like this, I like to keep it natural.

ingredients

30ml vegetable oil
175g onions – finely chopped
2 cloves garlic – finely grated
grated ginger (about the same
  volume as the garlic)
45ml water

350g chicken breast
2 good-sized ripe tomatoes
5ml butter to fry the tomatoes

Heat 30ml oil in the heavy-bottomed pan on a medium heat. While the oil is heating up, finely chop the onion.

When the oil is hot, add the chopped onion to the pan and stir fry for 5 minutes. The onions should not brown, so lower the heat a little if they start to fry too hard.

While the onions are frying, grate the garlic and ginger onto a small plate but make sure to give the onions a good stir from time to time so they don't

2.5ml ground coriander seed

2.5ml ground cumin seed

⅓ of a 2.5ml spoon **hot** chilli
  powder

½ a 2.5ml spoon turmeric

2 pinches ground cloves

2 pinches ground cardamom
  seeds

2 pinches ground mace (or
  ground nutmeg)

15ml Greek-style full-fat yoghurt

10ml tomato paste

2 grinds of black peppercorns

salt to taste

[optional] 2 pinches sugar
  (might be needed if your
  tomatoes are not perfectly
  ripe)

2 pinches dried fenugreek
  (*kasuri methi*) leaves

30ml double cream

30ml butter cut into smallish
  chunks

water to loosen the sauce

kitchen equipment

hand-held food grater with fine
  holes

potato masher

20cm heavy-bottomed pan

start browning.

Spoon the grated garlic and ginger into the pan (plus any juices left on the plate). Stir in well and stir fry continuously for 2 minutes.

Add 45ml water and mix in thoroughly.

Once the liquid starts to boil put a lid on the pan, turn the heat down to minimum and cook for 20 minutes. Do not remove the lid during this time.

While the onion mixture is cooking, skin the chicken breasts, remove any connective tissue and cut the meat into chunks about 25mm square.

Slide the tomatoes into a bowl of boiling water and leave for 2 minutes. Remove the tomatoes and plunge them into cold water. Dry the tomatoes, slice each one into quarters and peel off the skin. Remove the seeds and pith and then chop the tomato flesh into small chunks.

Heat a small frying pan on a medium heat. Melt 5ml butter in the frying pan and add the chopped tomatoes. Stir fry the tomatoes for about 5 minutes. Turn off the heat and use the potato masher to mash the tomato pieces into a purée. Set aside.

When the onion mixture is cooked, take the pan off the heat and remove the lid. Now use the potato masher to thoroughly mash the onions, garlic and ginger until you get a fairly smooth purée.

Return the pan to the heat, still at its lowest setting, and add the ground coriander, ground cumin, chilli powder, turmeric, ground cloves, ground cardamom seeds and ground mace.

Warm through the spices for about 1 minute, stirring all the time.

small frying pan

Raise the heat to medium and add the chicken chunks. Stir until the pieces of chicken have turned white over most of their surface.

Spoon the yoghurt into the pan and stir to mix. Be careful not to overheat the yoghurt or it will split.

Add the reserved puréed tomatoes, tomato paste, black pepper, salt, sugar [if using] and 30ml water. Stir to mix all the ingredients and bring the mixture to a simmer.

Simmer the chicken for 15 minutes (less if you used small chunks).

If the mixture starts getting a little dry add another 15ml water. Make sure the sauce is quite thick before you add the cream and the butter.

5 minutes before the chicken is ready add the dried fenugreek leaves and stir to mix.

2 minutes before the end of the cooking, make sure the sauce is quite dry then add the double cream. Stir to mix and gently re-heat the sauce.

1 minute before the chicken is ready add the chunks of butter and very gently heat through, stirring all the time. Do NOT bring the sauce to a boil or the butter will split.

Check that the chicken is thoroughly cooked and serve.

Balti

As the name suggests this dish is made in the balti style. The recipe isn't a copy of an authentic balti dish like the ones you would get in Birmingham's "Balti Triangle" but nevertheless it does have that special balti feel about it. It is strongly spiced but not particularly hot.

Balti dishes are cooked in a balti pan or karahi, which is like a Chinese wok but with two semi-circular handles instead of one long one. If you have a couple of small balti dishes that take one serving then warm them in the oven while you are cooking and use them to serve the dish at the table. It does give an authentic Balti House look to your meal. My recipe starts by making the sauce in a regular pan but the main cooking is done in a karahi, just as it should be.

In the Birmingham balti houses your balti will come served with the most enormous, puffy, buttery naan bread you've ever seen. Tear off a piece of naan, curl it up in your right hand and scoop out some Balti Chicken from your own individual pot. That's the way to do it!

We can't make naan bread that size at home without a tandoor but you could use shop-bought naan or follow my recipe for *griddled* Naan.

ingredients

45ml vegetable oil
1 whole black cardamom pod
25mm piece of cassia bark
200g onions – finely chopped
2 cloves garlic – finely grated
grated ginger (about half the
   volume of the garlic)
45ml water

350g chicken breast
half a medium onion (about
   75g trimmed weight)

Heat 45ml oil in a 20cm, heavy-bottomed pan on a medium heat. While the oil is heating up, finely chop the onion.

When the oil is hot, add the black cardamom pod and the cassia bark and stir so they are coated in oil. Now add the chopped onion to the pan and stir fry for 5 minutes. The onions should not brown, so lower the heat a little if they start to fry too hard.

While the onions are frying, grate the garlic and ginger onto a small plate but make sure to give the onions a good stir from time to time so they don't start browning.

2.5ml vegetable oil to fry the
   onion strips

5ml ground coriander seed
5ml ground cumin seed
5ml paprika
2.5ml *hot* chilli powder
2.5ml turmeric
2 pinches ground cloves

15ml tomato paste
2.5ml English mint sauce
   (preferably Colman's)
2 grinds of black peppercorns
salt to taste

water to loosen the sauce
[optional] 5ml ghee or
   vegetable oil

2 pinches dried fenugreek
   (*kasuri methi*) leaves

kitchen equipment

hand-held food grater with fine
   holes
potato masher
20cm heavy-bottomed pan
karahi or wok
rubber spatula

Spoon the grated garlic and ginger into the pan (plus any juices left on the plate). Stir in well and stir fry continuously for 2 minutes.

Add 45ml water and mix in thoroughly.

Once the liquid starts to boil put a lid on the pan, turn the heat down to minimum and cook for 20 minutes. Do not remove the lid during this time.

While the onion mixture is cooking, skin the chicken breasts, remove any connective tissue and cut the meat into chunks about 25mm square.

Place the onion half, cut-side down, on a chopping board and cut it into slices about 3-4mm across. Then cut the slices in half crossways so you get lots of short strips.

When the onion mixture is cooked, take the pan off the heat and remove the lid. Take out the cassia bark and the black cardamom pod and set aside. Now take a potato masher and thoroughly mash the onions, garlic and ginger until you get a fairly smooth purée. Set aside the pan for the moment – the rest of the cooking now takes place in the karahi.

Heat the karahi on a medium-high heat and add 2.5ml oil. Once the oil is hot add the onion strips and stir fry until they start to turn an even brown all over but without the edges burning.

Turn the heat to low and pour the onion purée from the other pan into the karahi. Scrape out every last drop of onion purée with a rubber spatula so you don't waste any.

Add the ground coriander, ground cumin, paprika, chilli powder, turmeric, ground cloves and the reserved cassia bark and black cardamom pod. Try to make sure the ground spices hit the onion purée and not the hot sides of the karahi or there is a risk your spices will burn.

Warm through the spices for about 1 minute, stirring all the time to mix them in thoroughly.

Raise the heat to medium and add the chicken chunks. Stir until the pieces of chicken have turned white over most of their surface.

Add the tomato paste, mint sauce, black pepper, salt and 45ml water. Stir to mix all the ingredients and bring the mixture to a simmer.

Simmer the chicken for 15minutes (less if you used small chunks)

If the mixture starts getting a little dry add 15ml water – no more just yet. As the chicken is cooking, add more water if the sauce gets too dry but, again, only 15ml at a time. If you like your curries very rich you could add 5ml ghee or vegetable oil to loosen the curry instead of 5ml water.

5 minutes before the chicken is ready add the dried fenugreek leaves and stir to mix.

Check that the chicken is thoroughly cooked and remove the cassia bark and black cardamom pod. Serve with naan bread.

Garlic Chicken

Garlic Chicken is a stir-fry with plenty of garlic, fresh tasting tomato, courgette and dark green coriander leaves.

Please don't cut down on the garlic; the dish won't taste right. If the amount of garlic is too much for you then it's best to choose another of the stir-fry recipes instead.

If you have a cast-iron sizzle platter, heat it up in the oven and serve the Garlic Chicken sizzling at the table. The dish looks very attractive and colourful with the strips of courgette and tomato surrounding the chicken.

ingredients

30ml vegetable oil
1 dried bay leaf
150g onions – finely chopped
2 cloves garlic – finely grated
grated ginger (about the same
   the volume as the garlic)
45ml water

350g chicken breast
2 garlic cloves cut into strips
   (see method)
2 good-sized tomatoes
100g of trimmed courgette (see
   method)
vegetable oil to cook the garlic
   and courgette strips (see
   method for amounts)

5ml ground coriander seed
2.5ml ground cumin seed
2.5ml *hot* chilli powder

Heat 30ml oil in the heavy-bottomed pan on a medium heat. While the oil is heating up, finely chop the onion.

When the oil is hot, add the bay leaf and stir to coat it in oil. Then add the chopped onion to the pan and stir fry for 5 minutes. The onions should not brown, so lower the heat a little if they start to fry too hard.

While the onions are frying, grate the garlic (the first 2 cloves) and ginger onto a small plate but make sure to give the onions a good stir from time to time so they don't start browning.

Spoon the grated garlic and ginger into the pan (plus any juices left on the plate). Stir in well and stir fry continuously for 2 minutes.

Add 45ml water and mix in thoroughly.

Once the liquid starts to boil put a lid on the pan, turn the heat down to minimum and cook for 20 minutes. Do not remove the lid during this time.

While the onion mixture is cooking, skin the chicken breasts, remove any connective tissue and cut the

½ a 2.5ml spoon of turmeric

2 pinches ground cardamom
    seeds

2.5ml lemon juice

3 grinds of black peppercorns

salt to taste

water to loosen the sauce

10ml finely chopped, fresh
    coriander leaves

kitchen equipment

hand-held food grater with fine
    holes

potato masher

20cm heavy-bottomed pan

karahi or wok

[optional] sizzle platter to serve

meat into chunks about 25mm square.

Peel and trim the additional 2 cloves of garlic. Slice the garlic cloves crossways and then cut each slice into strips.

Heat the karahi over a medium heat and add 2.5ml oil. Tip the garlic slices into the karahi and stir fry until the edges of the garlic strips are beginning to turn brown. Don't brown the garlic too much or it will end up tasting bitter. Now quickly remove the garlic slices from the karahi and transfer to a plate. Set aside. Wipe the karahi with kitchen paper to remove any garlic pieces and leftover oil.

Slide the tomatoes into a bowl of boiling water and leave for 2 minutes. Remove the tomatoes and plunge them into cold water. Dry the tomatoes, slice each one into quarters and peel off the skin. Remove the seeds and pith and then slice the tomato flesh into strips about 6mm wide. Set aside.

Top and tail the courgette. Slice it into quarters lengthways. Take a courgette quarter and cut out the seed area so you're left with a crescent of flesh and skin. Slice the courgette quarter diagonally into strips about 5mm wide. Repeat for the other quarters. You need about 100g of courgette strips for this dish.

When the onion mixture is cooked, take the pan off the heat and remove the lid. Remove the bay leaf and set aside. Now take a potato masher and thoroughly mash the onions, garlic and ginger until you get a fairly smooth purée.

Return the pan to the heat, still at its lowest setting, and add the ground coriander, ground cumin, chilli powder, turmeric and ground cardamom seeds.

Warm through the spices for about 1 minute, stirring all the time.

Raise the heat to medium and add the chicken chunks. Stir until the pieces of chicken have turned white over most of their surface. Return the bay leaf to the pan.

Add the fried garlic strips, lemon juice, black pepper and salt. Stir to mix all the ingredients and bring the mixture to a simmer.

Simmer the chicken for 15 minutes (less if you used small chunks).

If the mixture starts getting a little dry add 15ml water. There should only be a coating sauce left at the end of the cooking so be careful not to add too much water.

About 7 minutes before the chicken is ready, heat 2.5ml oil in the karahi over a high heat. When the oil is hot, tip the strips of courgette into the karahi and stir fry for about 3 minutes until the courgette pieces start to turn a little brown at the edges. At that point slide the tomato strips into the karahi, turn off the heat and stir the tomato and courgette strips together to just warm through the pieces of tomato. Leave the tomato and courgette strips in the karahi to stay warm until you need them.

2 minutes before the chicken is ready add 10ml finely chopped coriander leaves to the sauce and stir to mix.

Check that the chicken is thoroughly cooked and discard the bay leaf. Serve the chicken with its coating sauce on a hot sizzle platter (if using) and arrange the strips of tomato and courgette around the chicken.

Chicken with Tomatoes and Coriander

Chicken with Tomatoes and Coriander is a light, refreshing dish which is quite different from the standard restaurant curries. Tomatoes and coriander leaves go so well together and the flavours are brought out even more by the zingy flavour of the ground cardamom seeds.

The chunks of tomato are cooked quickly in a hot karahi to bring out their flavour. The method also helps the tomatoes to keep their texture and avoid being broken down into a purée.

This is a superb dish and well worth making for a dinner party or a special guest. Chicken with Tomatoes and Coriander is especially good to serve to people who are not keen on the heavier style of restaurant curries.

ingredients

30ml vegetable oil
175g onions – finely chopped
2 cloves garlic – finely grated
grated ginger (about the same
　volume as the garlic)
45ml water

350g chicken breast
3 good-sized tomatoes

7.5ml ground coriander seed
2.5ml ground cumin seed
⅔ of a 2.5ml spoon **hot** chilli
　powder
2.5ml turmeric
3 pinches ground cardamom
　seeds

10ml tomato paste

Heat 30ml oil in the heavy-bottomed pan on a medium heat. While the oil is heating up, finely chop the onion.

When the oil is hot, add the chopped onion to the pan and stir fry for 5 minutes. The onions should not brown, so lower the heat a little if they start to fry too hard.

While the onions are frying, grate the garlic and ginger onto a small plate but make sure to give the onions a good stir from time to time so they don't start browning.

Spoon the grated garlic and ginger into the pan (plus any juices left on the plate). Stir in well and stir fry continuously for 2 minutes.

Add 45ml water and mix in thoroughly.

Once the liquid starts to boil put a lid on the pan, turn the heat down to minimum and cook for 20 minutes. Do not remove the lid during this time.

2 grinds of black peppercorns
salt to taste

water to loosen the sauce
15ml butter
20ml finely chopped coriander
leaves

more finely chopped coriander
leaves to garnish

kitchen equipment

hand-held food grater with fine
holes
potato masher
20cm heavy-bottomed pan
karahi or wok

While the onion mixture is cooking, skin the chicken breasts, remove any connective tissue and cut the meat into chunks about 25mm square.

Slide the tomatoes into a bowl of boiling water and leave for 2 minutes. Remove the tomatoes and plunge them into cold water. Dry the tomatoes, slice each one into quarters and peel off the skin. Remove the seeds and pith and then chop the tomato flesh into chunks about 8mm square. Set aside.

When the onion mixture is cooked, take the pan off the heat and remove the lid. Now take a potato masher and thoroughly mash the onions, garlic and ginger until you get a fairly smooth purée.

Return the pan to the heat, still at its lowest setting, and add the ground coriander, ground cumin, chilli powder, turmeric and ground cardamom seeds.

Warm through the spices for about 1 minute, stirring all the time to mix them in thoroughly.

Raise the heat to medium and add the chicken chunks. Stir until the pieces of chicken have turned white over most of their surface.

Add the tomato paste, black pepper, salt and 30ml water. Stir to mix all the ingredients and bring the mixture to a simmer.

Simmer the chicken for 15 minutes (less if you used small chunks).

If the mixture starts getting a little dry add 15ml water - you probably won't need any more. The sauce needs to be as dry as possible before you add the chopped tomatoes as they will give off some liquid.

While the chicken is cooking, heat a karahi over a high heat. When the karahi is hot, slide in 15ml butter and stir to melt. As soon as the butter melts add the chopped tomato pieces and stir fry for 2 minutes until the tomatoes have lost a lot of their liquid. Remove the karahi from the heat but leave the cooked tomato chunks in the karahi to keep warm.

2 minutes before the end of the cooking add the cooked tomato chunks and 20ml finely chopped coriander leaves to the pan. Stir to mix, taking care not to break up the tomato pieces.

Check that the chicken is thoroughly cooked. Serve garnished with finely chopped coriander leaves.

Satkara

Satkara (also sat kara, shatkora, hatkora) is the fruit of the tree *Citrus macroptera* which grows semi-wild in the Sylhet area of Bangladesh. Sometimes know as "wild lemon", the fruit is commonly used in pickles but is also cooked in some savoury Bangladeshi dishes.

Most of us will find it difficult to get hold of satkara unless we happened to have a Bangladeshi grocer's nearby, so in my recipe I have substituted regular lemons. This is another wonderfully hot, sweet and sour recipe and the heat comes from fresh green chillies rather than chilli powder. You can tone down the heat if you like and you will still be able to enjoy the fresh citrus flavour of the dish.

This is my interpretation of the dish served in Bangladeshi restaurants so it is by no means authentic, although it does taste good. Many restaurants use slices of satkara but I have tried this with regular lemon and the cooking time isn't long enough for the lemon rind to soften and it tastes unpleasantly harsh when you bite into it. So I have used lemon zest and lemon juice instead, with some lemon twists as a garnish.

ingredients

45ml vegetable oil
2 pinches kalonji seeds
200g onions – finely chopped
2 cloves garlic – finely grated
grated ginger (about the same
   volume as the garlic)
45ml water

350g chicken breast
4 – 8 long thin green chillies
the zest of a whole lemon –
   scraped off into thin strips

Heat 45ml oil in a 20cm, heavy-bottomed pan on a medium heat. While the oil is heating up, finely chop the onion.

When the oil is hot, add the kalonji and stir so the seeds are coated in oil. Now add the chopped onion to the pan and stir fry for 5 minutes. The onions should not brown, so lower the heat a little if they start to fry too hard.

While the onions and kalonji are frying, grate the garlic and ginger onto a small plate but make sure to give the onions a good stir from time to time so they don't start browning.

with a zester
30ml ground almonds

5ml ground coriander seed
2.5ml ground cumin seed
¾ of a 2.5ml spoon turmeric
2 pinches ground mace (or
    nutmeg)

5ml lemon juice
2.5ml sugar
2 grinds of black peppercorns
salt to taste

water to loosen the sauce

lemon twists to garnish (cut
    from a whole lemon)

kitchen equipment

hand-held food grater with fine
    holes
potato masher
20cm heavy-bottomed pan
lemon zester

Spoon the grated garlic and ginger into the pan (plus any juices left on the plate). Stir in well and stir fry continuously for 2 minutes.

Add 45ml water and mix in thoroughly.

Once the liquid starts to boil put a lid on the pan, turn the heat down to minimum and cook for 20 minutes. Do not remove the lid during this time.

While the onion mixture is cooking, skin the chicken breasts, remove any connective tissue and cut the meat into chunks about 25mm square.

Slice the stalks off the chillies and cut them in half lengthways. Remove the seeds and pith by sliding a teaspoon along the length of the chilli half. Set aside.

Using a lemon zester (or a fine grater) scrape off the zest from a lemon (make sure you leave the lemon whole to do this bit). Set aside the zest. Now cut the lemon in half and squeeze the juice into a bowl. Take another lemon and cut thin slices for the garnish. Cut each circular slice once from the centre to the edge and make a twist. Set aside.

When the onion mixture is cooked, take the pan off the heat and remove the lid. Now take a potato masher and thoroughly mash the onions, garlic and ginger until you get a fairly smooth purée.

Return the pan to the heat and add the ground almonds and lemon zest. Raise the heat a little to get things sizzling then turn the heat back to low and stir fry for 2 minutes.

Add the ground coriander, ground cumin, turmeric and ground mace.

Warm through the spices for about 1 minute, stirring all the time to mix them in thoroughly.

Raise the heat to medium and add the chicken chunks. Stir until the pieces of chicken have turned white over most of their surface.

Add the lemon juice, sugar, black pepper, salt and 45ml water. Stir to mix all the ingredients and bring the mixture to a simmer.

Simmer the chicken for 15 minutes (less if you used small chunks).

If the mixture starts getting a little dry add 15ml water – no more just yet. As the chicken is cooking, add more water if the sauce gets too dry but, again, only 15ml at a time.

10 minutes before the chicken is ready add the chilli halves and stir to mix. Poke down the chilli halves into the sauce so they cook completely and transfer their heat into the sauce.

Towards the end of the cooking taste the sauce and adjust the sweet/sour balance if you think it's not quite right by adding a little more lemon juice or a little more sugar. Also, check the heat is right. If your chillies were quite mild you may need to add a pinch or two of chilli powder. Remember to go carefully. You can always add a little more chilli powder but you can't take the heat out once it's gone in.

Check that the chicken is thoroughly cooked. Serve garnished with the twists of lemon.

Pudina Murgh

Pudina Murgh is chicken (*murgh*) flavoured with mint (*pudina*). Pudina Murgh is a piquant curry which uses herbs as well as spices for a full flavour. If you like the standard restaurant Patia I'm sure you'll enjoy this recipe too. It has a similar hot, sweet and sour taste but with the added freshness of the mint.

If you can't get hold of fresh mint leaves use 5ml English mint sauce instead but reduce the red wine vinegar by half.

ingredients

45ml vegetable oil
2 pinches kalonji seeds
200g onions – finely chopped
2 cloves garlic – finely grated
grated ginger (about the same
  volume as the garlic)
45ml water

350g chicken breast

5ml ground coriander seed
5ml ground cumin seed
⅔ of a 5ml spoon **hot** chilli
  powder
½ a 2.5ml spoon turmeric
2.5ml paprika
1 pinch ground cloves
3 pinches ground cardamom
  seeds

30ml Greek-style full fat yoghurt

Heat 45ml oil in the heavy-bottomed pan on a medium heat. While the oil is heating up, finely chop the onion.

When the oil is hot, add the kalonji and stir so the seeds are coated in oil. Now add the chopped onion to the pan and stir fry for 5 minutes. The onions should not brown, so lower the heat a little if they start to fry too hard.

While the onions are frying, grate the garlic and ginger onto a small plate but make sure to give the onions a good stir from time to time so they don't start browning.

Spoon the grated garlic and ginger into the pan (plus any juices left on the plate). Stir in well and stir fry continuously for 2 minutes.

Add 45ml water and mix in thoroughly.

Once the liquid starts to boil put a lid on the pan, turn the heat down to minimum and cook for 20 minutes. Do not remove the lid during this time.

While the onion mixture is cooking, skin the chicken breasts, remove any connective tissue and cut the

15ml finely chopped mint leaves

15ml tomato paste

2.5ml sugar

5ml red wine vinegar

2 grinds of black peppercorns

salt to taste

water to loosen the sauce

15ml butter

a few sprigs of mint leaves to
     garnish

kitchen equipment

hand-held food grater with fine
     holes

potato masher

20cm heavy-bottomed pan

meat into chunks about 25mm square.

When the onion mixture is cooked, take the pan off the heat and remove the lid. Now take a potato masher and thoroughly mash the onions, garlic and ginger until you get a fairly smooth purée.

Return the pan to the heat, still at its lowest setting, and add the ground coriander, ground cumin, chilli powder, turmeric, paprika, ground cloves and ground cardamom seeds.

Warm through the spices for about 1 minute, stirring all the time.

Raise the heat to medium and add the chicken chunks. Stir until the pieces of chicken have turned white over most of their surface.

Spoon the yoghurt into the pan and stir to mix. Be careful not to overheat the yoghurt or it will split.

Add the chopped mint leaves, tomato paste, sugar, wine vinegar, black pepper and salt. Stir to mix all the ingredients and bring the mixture to a simmer.

Simmer the chicken for 15 minutes (less if you used small chunks).

If the mixture starts getting a little dry add 15ml water – no more just yet. As the chicken is cooking add more water if the sauce gets too dry but, again, only 15ml at a time. Make sure the sauce is quite thick before you add the butter.

1 minute before the chicken is ready add the butter and very gently heat through, stirring all the time so the butter melts. Do NOT bring the sauce to a boil or the butter will split.

Check that the chicken is thoroughly cooked. Serve garnished with a few sprigs of mint leaves.

Chicken Shashlik Bhuna

Chicken Shashlik Bhuna is an inspired combination of two familiar restaurant dishes. A thick spicy bhuna sauce has been added to the chicken, pepper, tomato and onion pieces from the tandoor-cooked shashlik.

You won't find this dish on many restaurant menus but it was a speciality of Mr Miah and his team who used to run The Palm Tree restaurant near Reading. I have tried to make my recipe taste as similar to theirs as possible and I am pleased with the results. But not being able to cook the chicken and vegetables in a tandoor is quite a handicap towards achieving the same delicious smoky taste of the shashlik.

To compensate for the lack of tandoori taste, I have used smoked paprika instead of some or all of the chilli powder. Smoked paprika is often quite hot, unlike regular paprika. It does vary in heat so you may need to add extra chilli powder if your smoked paprika is on the mild side. A bhuna will usually have a medium heat and that is what you are trying to achieve.

In the restaurant, this dish comes served on a hot sizzle platter. You can recreate the same effect at home if you have your own cast-iron sizzle platters, which you should heat in the oven until very hot.

ingredients

30ml vegetable oil
175g onions – finely chopped
1 whole black cardamom pod
2 cloves garlic – finely grated
grated ginger (about half the
    volume of the garlic)
45ml water

half a medium-sized onion
    (about 75g trimmed weight)
75g green pepper (trimmed

Heat 30ml oil in the heavy-bottomed pan on a medium heat. While the oil is heating up, finely chop 175g onions.

When the oil is hot, add the black cardamom pod and stir to coat it in oil. Then add the chopped onion to the pan and stir fry for 5 minutes. The onions should not brown, so lower the heat a little if they start to fry too hard.

While the onions are frying, grate the garlic and ginger onto a small plate but make sure to give the onions a good stir from time to time so they don't

weight)

vegetable oil to baste the
vegetables

350g chicken breast

5ml ground coriander seed

5ml ground cumin seed

2.5ml turmeric

2.5ml smoked paprika

[optional] a few pinches of *hot*
chilli powder if your smoked
paprika lacks heat

2 pinches ground cloves

5ml tomato paste

2.5ml lemon juice

2 grinds of black peppercorns

salt to taste

water to loosen the sauce

2 medium-sized tomatoes (about
75g each)

2 pinches dried fenugreek
(*kasuri methi*) leaves

kitchen equipment

hand-held food grater with fine
holes

potato masher

20cm heavy-bottomed pan

2 long skewers (preferably
double pronged)

pastry brush

[optional] 2 single-portion cast-

start browning.

Spoon the grated garlic and ginger into the pan (plus any juices left on the plate). Stir in well and stir fry continuously for 2 minutes.

Add 45ml water and mix in thoroughly.

Once the liquid starts to boil put a lid on the pan, turn the heat down to minimum and cook for 20 minutes. Do not remove the lid during this time.

While the onion mixture is cooking, heat the grill in your cooker to medium-high. Cut 75g onions into large chunks about 25mm across. Thread the onion chunks onto one of the skewers. Take a green pepper, remove the seeds and pith and weigh out 75g. Cut the pepper into large chunks about 25mm across. Thread the pepper chunks onto the other skewer.

Take a pastry brush and liberally baste the onions and peppers with vegetable oil. Sit the skewers on your grill rack and place it under the hot grill. Turn the skewers from time to time until the edges of the onions and peppers are nicely charred. Set aside.

While the onions and peppers are grilling, skin the chicken breasts, remove any connective tissue and cut the meat into chunks about 25mm square.

When the onion mixture is cooked, take the pan off the heat and remove the lid. Remove the black cardamom pod and set aside. Now take a potato masher and mash the onions, garlic and ginger until you get a fairly smooth purée.

Return the pan to the heat, still at its lowest setting, and add the ground coriander, ground cumin, turmeric, smoked paprika, [optional] chilli powder and ground cloves.

Warm through the spices for about 1 minute, stirring all the time to mix them in thoroughly. Return the

iron sizzle platters
rubber spatula

black cardamom pod to the pan.

Raise the heat to medium and add the chicken chunks. Stir until the pieces of chicken have turned white over most of their surface.

Add the tomato paste, lemon juice, black pepper, salt and 30ml water. Stir to mix all the ingredients and bring the mixture to a simmer.

Cook the chicken for 15 minutes (less if you used small chunks).

If the mixture starts getting a little dry add just 10ml water. This dish has a thick coating sauce so be careful how much water you add. Only add more water if the sauce is beginning to fry in the pan.

Re-heat your grill to maximum and cut the tomatoes in half. Sit the tomato halves on the grill rack, skin side up, and place under the hot grill. Grill the tomatoes until the skins go black on the top. Place the cooked onion and pepper chunks in the grill area to warm through. Turn off the heat to the grill and leave the tomatoes, onions and peppers in the grill area to keep warm.

5 minutes before the end of the cooking add the dried fenugreek leaves to the sauce and stir to mix. Place the cast-iron sizzle platters (if using) in a hot oven.

Check that the chicken is thoroughly cooked. Remove the black cardamom pod and discard.

Transfer the chicken and its sauce to the hot sizzle platters or a warm serving dish. Remove every last bit of sauce from the pan with a rubber spatula. Arrange the onion and pepper chunks over the chicken. Remove the skins from the tomato halves and cut each half into 3 wedges. Arrange the tomato wedges over the chicken. Serve.

Chicken with Coconut

I was at a food exhibition a few years ago and I came across a stand hosted by the Spices Board of India. There was a cooking demonstration at the stand organised by chefs from the Malabar Junction restaurant in London. The Malabar Junction specialises in the South Indian food of Kerala and the dishes they were offering were absolutely delicious and quite different from normal restaurant fare.

This recipe is my take on that style of curry. The curry is moderately hot but the heat is tempered by the sweetness of the coconut milk in the sauce. The sauce is not as thick as regular Indian restaurant curries but that's the norm for this type of curry. Don't forget the garnish of toasted coconut – the crunchy coconut flakes are a perfect contrast to the rich, silky sauce.

ingredients

45ml vegetable oil
200g onions – finely chopped
30mm piece cassia bark
2 cloves garlic – finely grated
grated ginger (about same
    volume as the garlic)
45ml water

350g chicken breast
20ml desiccated coconut

5ml ground coriander seed
2.5ml ground cumin seed
2.5ml *hot* chilli powder
2.5ml turmeric
3 pinches ground cloves
4 pinches ground dry roasted
    fennel seeds

Heat 45ml oil in the heavy-bottomed pan on a medium heat. While the oil is heating up, finely chop the onion.

When the oil is hot, add the piece of cassia bark and stir to coat it in oil. Then add the chopped onion to the pan and stir fry for 5 minutes. The onions should not brown, so lower the heat a little if they start to fry too hard.

While the onions are frying, grate the garlic and ginger onto a small plate but make sure to give the onions a good stir from time to time so they don't start browning.

Spoon the grated garlic and ginger into the pan (plus any juices left on the plate). Stir in well and stir fry continuously for 2 minutes.

Add 45ml water and mix in thoroughly.

Once the liquid starts to boil put a lid on the pan, turn

5ml tomato paste

2.5ml lime juice

2 grinds of black peppercorns

salt to taste

90ml tinned coconut milk (shake
  the tin well before you open it)

kitchen equipment

hand-held food grater with fine
  holes

potato masher

20cm heavy-bottomed pan

small frying pan

spatula

pestle and mortar

the heat down to minimum and cook for 20 minutes.
Do not remove the lid during this time.

While the onion mixture is cooking, skin the chicken
breasts, remove any connective tissue and cut the
meat into chunks about 25mm square.

Heat a small frying pan (without any oil) on a medium-
low heat and sprinkle in the desiccated coconut. Keep
stirring the coconut with a spatula while it is toasting.
The coconut is done when the pieces have turned
golden brown. Transfer the coconut onto a plate and
set aside.

Dry roast some fennel seeds, cool on a plate and
grind with a pestle and mortar as best you can. A
medium/coarse grind is what you're aiming for.

When the onion mixture is cooked, take the pan off
the heat and remove the lid. Remove the cassia bark
and set aside. Now take a potato masher and
thoroughly mash the onions, garlic and ginger until
you get a fairly smooth purée.

Return the pan to the heat, still at its lowest setting,
and add the ground coriander, ground cumin, chilli
powder, turmeric, ground cloves and ground dry
roasted fennel seeds.

Warm through the spices for about 1 minute, stirring
all the time. Return the cassia bark to the pan.

Raise the heat to medium and add the chicken
chunks. Stir until the pieces of chicken have turned
white over most of their surface.

Add the tomato paste, lime juice, black pepper, salt
and 45ml coconut milk. Stir to mix and bring the
mixture to a simmer.

Simmer the chicken for 15 minutes (less if you used
small chunks).

Once the mixture starts getting quite thick, add a further 15ml coconut milk. Add the rest of the coconut milk, 15ml at a time, while the chicken is cooking. Bring the sauce back to a simmer by temporarily raising the heat each time you add more liquid. If you add the whole 90ml of coconut milk at the beginning you won't be able to reduce down the liquid without boiling it vigorously which will ruin the sauce and make the chicken quite tough.

Remove the cassia bark. Check that the chicken is thoroughly cooked and serve garnished with the toasted coconut.

Subzi Murgh

Subzi Murgh means chicken with vegetables so it's a general name for all sorts of dishes, with the vegetables varying from recipe to recipe. In my recipe the main vegetables are onions and tomatoes, along with green herbs in the form of fresh coriander leaves.

The sauce is richly flavoured with warm spices like cassia and cloves. The dish looks especially attractive when served with a garnish of more fresh coriander leaves and would be very impressive served as part of a dinner party meal.

ingredients

45ml vegetable oil
25mm piece of cassia bark
200g onions – finely chopped
2 cloves garlic – finely grated
grated ginger (about the same
  the volume as the garlic)
45ml water

350g chicken breast
2 good-sized tomatoes
½ a medium onion (about 75g
  trimmed weight) – sliced as in
  method
5ml vegetable oil to fry the
  onion slices

5ml ground coriander seed
5ml ground cumin seed
⅔ of a 2.5ml spoon **hot** chilli
  powder
2.5ml turmeric

Heat 45ml oil in a heavy-bottomed pan on a medium heat. While the oil is heating up, finely chop the onion.

When the oil is hot add the piece of cassia bark and stir to coat it in oil. Now add the chopped onion to the pan and stir fry for 5 minutes. The onions should not brown, so lower the heat a little if they start to fry too hard.

While the onions are frying, grate the garlic and ginger onto a small plate but make sure to give the onions a good stir from time to time so they don't start browning.

Spoon the grated garlic and ginger into the pan (plus any juices left on the plate). Stir in well and stir fry continuously for 2 minutes.

Add 45ml water and mix in thoroughly.

Once the liquid starts to boil put a lid on the pan, turn the heat down to minimum and cook for 20 minutes. Do not remove the lid during this time.

2.5ml paprika

3 pinches ground cloves

10ml tomato paste

2.5ml lemon juice

[optional] 2 pinches sugar if
your tomatoes are not
perfectly ripe

2 grinds of black peppercorns

salt to taste

water to loosen the sauce

15ml finely chopped coriander
leaves

more finely chopped coriander
leaves to garnish

kitchen equipment

hand-held food grater with fine
holes

potato masher

20cm heavy-bottomed pan

karahi or wok

While the onion mixture is cooking, skin the chicken breasts, remove any connective tissue and cut the meat into chunks about 25mm square.

Slide the tomatoes into a bowl of boiling water and leave for 2 minutes. Remove the tomatoes and plunge them into cold water. Dry the tomatoes, slice each one into quarters and peel off the skin. Remove the seeds and pith and then chop the tomato flesh into chunks about 8mm square. Set aside.

Place the onion-half, cut-side down, on a chopping board and cut it into slices about 3-4mm across. Then cut the slices in half crossways so you get lots of short strips.

Heat a karahi on a medium-high heat and add 5ml oil. Once the oil is hot add the onion strips and stir fry until they start to turn light brown all over but without the edges burning (about 4 minutes). Transfer the onion strips to a plate.

Place the chopped tomatoes in the karahi and stir fry for 1 minute. Transfer the tomato chunks to another plate and set aside.

When the onion mixture is cooked, take the pan off the heat and remove the lid. Remove the cassia bark and set aside. Now take a potato masher and thoroughly mash the onions, garlic and ginger until you get a fairly smooth purée.

Return the pan to the heat, still at its lowest setting, and add the ground coriander, ground cumin, chilli powder, turmeric, paprika and ground cloves.

Warm through the spices for about 1 minute, stirring all the time. Return the piece of cassia bark to the pan.

Raise the heat to medium and add the chicken chunks. Stir until the pieces of chicken have turned white over most of their surface.

Add the tomato paste, lemon juice, sugar (if using), black pepper, salt and 30ml water. Stir to mix all the ingredients and bring the mixture to a simmer.

Simmer the chicken for 15 minutes (less if you used small chunks).

If the sauce starts getting a little dry add 15ml water – you probably won't need any more. Make sure the sauce is quite thick before you add the tomatoes because they will add a lot of liquid to the sauce.

10 minutes before the end of the cooking, add the fried onion slices and stir to mix.

3 minutes before the chicken is ready, add 15ml finely chopped coriander leaves and the fried tomato chunks. Stir to mix, being careful not to break up the tomato chunks too much.

Check that the chicken is thoroughly cooked. Remove the cassia bark and discard. Serve garnished with more finely chopped coriander leaves.

King Prawn Sizzler

King Prawn Sizzler is a stir-fry dish with only a coating sauce. I'm not a big fan of prawn curries where little prawns are drowned in a sea of sauce but a stir-fry dish like this using plump king prawns cooked with fresh onions, peppers and tomatoes looks and tastes delicious.

Like all stir-fries you need to prepare the ingredients in advance. Once you start cooking there isn't much time to continue the preparation. Once you do start cooking the dish is very quick to make.

It's essential to use raw prawns which will be grey in colour and almost translucent. Ready-cooked prawns (which will be pink) will not work for this recipe as they will overcook and become tough and very chewy. If your prawns are frozen allow them to defrost slowly in the fridge until they are completely thawed. Frying the prawns first in just a little oil will give them a wonderful taste and attractive brown patches on the sides. If you use ready-cooked prawns they will have been previously boiled and you will never get the sweet taste and succulent texture you get from frying raw prawns.

If you have a cast-iron sizzle platter with a wooden stand then use it to serve the King Prawn Sizzler, just as they would in an Indian restaurant.

ingredients

225g raw peeled jumbo king prawns – thawed if previously frozen

2 good-sized tomatoes

½ a large onion (about 100g trimmed weight)

75g red pepper (trimmed weight)

1 clove garlic – finely grated

grated ginger (about the same volume as the garlic)

Slide the tomatoes into a bowl of boiling water and leave for 2 minutes. Remove the tomatoes and plunge them into cold water. Dry the tomatoes, slice each one into quarters and peel off the skin. Remove the seeds and pith and then chop the tomato flesh into chunks about 5mm square. Set aside.

Place the half of onion, cut-side down, on a chopping board and cut it into thick slices about 8mm wide. Then cut the slices in half crossways so you get lots of short strips. Slice 75g red pepper into strips about the same length and width as the longer onion strips you've just cut.

vegetable oil (see method for
   amounts at each stage)

2.5ml ground coriander seed
2.5ml ground cumin seed
½ a 2.5ml spoon *hot* chilli
   powder
½ a 2.5ml spoon turmeric
2 pinches ground cardamom
   seeds
2 pinches ground cloves

2.5ml lemon juice
2 grinds of black peppercorns
salt to taste
3 pinches sugar

water to loosen the coating
   sauce
10ml finely chopped coriander
   leaves

more finely chopped coriander
   leaves to garnish

kitchen equipment

hand-held food grater with fine
   holes
karahi or wok
[optional] cast-iron sizzle platter
   to serve

Make sure the peeled jumbo king prawns are completely defrosted (if previously frozen). Dry the prawns thoroughly with kitchen paper.

Finely chop the coriander leaves and grate the garlic and ginger onto a plate. Measure out the ground coriander seeds, ground cumin seeds, chilli powder, turmeric, ground cardamom seeds and ground cloves onto another plate.

Pour 2.5ml vegetable oil into the karahi and place on a medium heat. When the oil is hot slide in the pepper strips and stir fry for about 2 minutes by which time the peppers should start to show small brown patches on the skin. Remove the pepper slices from the karahi and set aside. Raise the heat to medium-high.

Divide the prawns into 2 batches. Take the first batch of prawns and toss them into the hot karahi. Stir fry for 2 minutes or until the prawns have turned pink on the outside and white in the middle. Remove the first batch of prawns from the karahi and set aside on a large plate.

Add half a 2.5ml spoon of oil to the karahi. When the oil is hot stir fry the second batch of prawns in the same way as the first. When done, transfer the second batch of prawns onto the plate along with the first batch. Set aside.

Now add 5ml oil to the karahi and keep on a medium-high heat. When the oil is hot slide in the onion strips and stir fry until they start to turn an even brown all over but without the edges burning – about 3 minutes.

Remove the karahi from the heat to let it cool down a little. Turn the heat down to low.

Pour 15ml oil into the karahi and return it to the heat.

When the oil is hot, spoon the grated garlic and

ginger into the karahi. Stir fry on low heat for about 30 seconds.

Now add the chopped tomatoes and stir fry for about 1 minute. Add 10ml water and mix in with the tomatoes.

Carefully tip the ground spices into the karahi. Try and make sure they land on the tomato mixture and not the sides of the karahi or there is a risk that the spices will burn.

Stir the ground spices into the tomato mixture and warm them through for about 1 minute, stirring frequently.

Add the lemon juice, black pepper, salt, sugar and 45ml water to the karahi and stir to mix.

Bring the mixture to a gentle simmer and add the reserved pepper and onion strips. Simmer gently for about 10 minutes.

If the sauce starts to get too thick it will burn on the bottom of the karahi, so add 15ml water if all the moisture has evaporated. Repeat if necessary during the cooking but only add 15ml water at a time. Be careful how much extra water you add; too much and you'll get a sloppy wet sauce, too little and the sauce will form unattractive lumps.

When the 10 minutes simmering is up add 10ml chopped coriander leaves and the reserved prawns. Return the sauce to barely a simmer and cook for about 3 minutes or until the prawns have heated right through.

The sauce should now be nice and glossy around the prawns, peppers and onions.

Serve in a hot cast-iron sizzle platter (if using) garnished with more chopped coriander leaves.

Lamb Koftas

It's not often you see koftas on Indian restaurant menus but when you do they're often extremely good and very different from your average curry house fare.

Koftas are spicy little meatballs which are usually served plain as a starter or with a sauce for a main meal. This recipe is for a main meal kofta curry but you can easily omit the sauce and serve the koftas just as they are as a snack.

If you want to experiment you can make the sauce from just about any of the other House Specials in this book and try combining it with the koftas. I particularly like using the Tamarind Chicken recipe and replacing the chicken with the koftas.

This recipe takes longer to cook than the other curry recipes and it might take just over an hour to make unless you work very quickly. It does need a bit more work but when you bite into a soft, spicy meatball covered with the creamy sauce I think you'll find it's worth it.

ingredients

for the curry base:

45ml vegetable oil
1 dried bay leaf
200g onions – finely chopped
2 cloves garlic – finely grated
grated ginger (about half the
   volume of the garlic)
45ml water

for the koftas:

350g lean minced lamb (ideally
   about 10% fat but 20% fat
   maximum)
30ml Greek-style full fat yoghurt
2.5ml grated ginger

Heat 45ml oil in a 20cm, heavy-bottomed pan on a medium heat. While the oil is heating up, finely chop the onion.

When the oil is hot, add the bay leaf and stir to coat it in oil. Then add the chopped onion to the pan and stir fry for 5 minutes. The onions should not brown, so lower the heat a little if they start to fry too hard.

While the onions are frying, grate the garlic and ginger onto a small plate but make sure to give the onions a good stir from time to time so they don't start browning.

Spoon the grated garlic and ginger into the pan (plus any juices left on the plate). Stir in well and stir fry continuously for 2 minutes.

2.5ml ground cumin seeds

⅓ of a 2.5ml spoon *hot* chilli powder

3 pinches ground cinnamon

3 pinches ground mace (or nutmeg)

3 grinds black peppercorns

salt (use plenty)

for the sauce:

5ml ground coriander seed

5ml ground cumin seed

½ a 2.5ml spoon *hot* chilli powder

½ a 2.5ml spoon turmeric

3 pinches ground cardamom seeds

30ml Greek-style full fat yoghurt

10ml tomato paste

2 grinds of black peppercorns

salt to taste

water to loosen the sauce

10ml finely chopped coriander leaves

more finely chopped coriander leaves to garnish

kitchen equipment

hand-held food grater with fine holes

potato masher

20cm heavy-bottomed pan

Add 45ml water and mix in thoroughly.

Once the liquid starts to boil put a lid on the pan, turn the heat down to minimum and cook for 20 minutes. Do not remove the lid during this time.

While the onion mixture is cooking, make the meatballs. Take a large bowl and put in all the ingredients for the meatballs.

Mix all the ingredients together with a fork, breaking up as many lumps of minced lamb as possible. Then finish off mixing the ingredients thoroughly with your hands.

Now take a portion of the meatball mixture about the size of a walnut. Roll the mixture into a ball between the palms of your hands. Do not compress the meatball too much but just enough for everything to hold together. Place your meatball on a plate and work your way through the mixture to get about 16 koftas (one or two more or less is fine).

When the onion mixture is cooked, take the pan off the heat and remove the lid. Remove the bay leaf and set aside. Now take a potato masher and mash the onions, garlic and ginger until you get a fairly smooth purée.

Return the pan to the heat, still at its lowest setting, and add the ground coriander, ground cumin, chilli powder, turmeric and ground cardamom seeds.

Warm through the spices for about 1 minute, stirring all the time to mix them in thoroughly. Return the bay leaf to the pan.

Add 30ml Greek-style yoghurt and stir until the yoghurt has blended with the onion and spice mixture. Now add the tomato paste, black pepper, salt and 15ml water.

Stir to mix all the ingredients and bring the mixture to

large (28cm) frying pan

a simmer. Simmer the sauce for 15 minutes, stirring from time to time.

If the mixture starts getting a little dry add 15ml water – no more just yet. Add more water if the sauce gets too dry but, again, just 15ml at a time.

While the sauce is cooking fry the meatballs.

Take a large frying pan and just coat the surface with a little vegetable oil. A good way to do this is to pour some oil onto a wad of kitchen paper and wipe the oiled paper around the surface of the frying pan. Heat the frying pan over a medium-high heat.

When the frying pan is hot roll the meatballs off their plate into the pan. Try not to use a spatula to turn the meatballs (at least at first) or they may break up. The best way is to lift the frying pan and gently roll it around in a circular motion so the meatballs roll over with a new face touching the pan. Turn the meatballs frequently and cook for about 15 minutes so they are ready at about the same time as the sauce. If the meatballs are browning too fast reduce the heat a little.

If you used 20% fat minced lamb a fair amount of fat will accumulate in the frying pan. From time to time either spoon off the fat or mop it up with a wad of kitchen paper (be careful not to touch the pan with your fingers).

When the meatballs are cooked right through, remove them from the frying pan and place them on a plate that is covered with kitchen paper. Roll the meatballs around to soak up as much fat as possible.

When the sauce has finished simmering remove the bay leaf, add 10ml finely chopped coriander leaves and stir to mix. If the sauce is too thick adjust the consistency with a little more water and stir to mix.

Now transfer the meatballs to the sauce.

Gently stir the meatballs so they are covered with sauce. Use an ordinary metal tablespoon to stir the meatballs because a thick wooden or plastic spoon might damage them.

Cook the meatballs in the sauce on a low heat for about 5 minutes to allow the flavours to blend together.

Serve in a shallow dish garnished with finely chopped coriander leaves.

Curry House Favourites

I have chosen 12 of the most popular curries on the Indian restaurant menu for this chapter. All the curries appeared in The Curry House Cookery Book but the method was much more complicated in order to duplicate the restaurant experience. A curry base and spice mixes had to be made in advance and the meat and rice had to be pre-cooked. The recipes all took far longer than an hour to make.

The recipes for the curry house favourites included here have been rewritten so the method is much simpler and the curries can be made in under an hour. Most importantly though, the recipes have been completely revised to reflect how I like to make them myself these days. There are, of course, many more standard curries served in Indian restaurants, but the 12 I have chosen offer a good selection, ranging from mild to hot and from creamy to sweet and sour.

Because I have simplified the method, you should not expect the curries to turn out like the ones you'll find in restaurants. However, they are still most definitely in the restaurant style. What the recipes don't have is the excessive amounts of oil and salt that you find in far too many restaurant curries. Nor do the curries in this book contain any artificial colouring to make them look more appetising. They look good just on their own.

The curries in this chapter turn out like a cross between restaurant curries and the ready-meal curries you can buy in British supermarkets. The big difference is that I am usually disappointed when I eat supermarket ready meals. I always expect them to taste like restaurant curries but they never do. These recipes bridge the gap with less than an hour's work.

Rogan Josh

Rogan Josh is a traditional dish but it does have considerable regional variations in style.

For example, Kashmiri Rogan Josh is quite different from Punjabi Rogan Josh. Kashmiri Rogan Josh does not use onions or garlic and uses only powdered ginger, not fresh. Punjabi Rogan Josh, on the other hand, does indeed use fresh onions, garlic and ginger. One thing all the traditional variations of Rogan Josh have in common is that they are made with lamb or, more commonly, mutton.

The restaurant Rogan Josh, on the other hand, can be made with chicken or prawns as well as lamb. It is usually served medium in heat and is rich in tomatoes and coriander leaves. In Indian restaurants, the name of the dish is often shortened to just Rogan.

ingredients

45ml vegetable oil
25mm piece cassia bark
2 pinches fennel seeds
200g onions – finely chopped
2 cloves garlic – finely grated
grated ginger (about equal the
    volume of the garlic)
45ml water

350g chicken breast

5ml ground coriander seed
5ml ground cumin seed
2.5ml **hot** chilli powder
2.5ml turmeric
5ml paprika
3 pinches ground cloves

Heat 45ml oil in the heavy-bottomed pan on a medium heat. While the oil is heating up, finely chop the onion.

When the oil is hot, add the cassia bark and fennel seeds and stir to coat them in oil. Then add the chopped onions and stir fry for 5 minutes. The onions should not brown, so lower the heat a little if they start to fry too hard.

While the onions are frying, grate the garlic and ginger onto a small plate but make sure to give the onions a good stir from time to time so they don't start browning.

Spoon the grated garlic and ginger into the pan (plus any juices left on the plate). Stir in well and stir fry continuously for 2 minutes.

Add 45ml water and mix in thoroughly.

20ml tomato paste

2 grinds of black peppercorns

salt to taste

water to loosen the sauce

1 good-sized tomato

5ml butter to fry the tomato

10ml butter to enrich the sauce

15ml finely chopped coriander
  leaves

a sprinkling of finely chopped
  coriander leaves to garnish

kitchen equipment

hand-held food grater with fine
  holes

potato masher

20cm heavy-bottomed pan

Once the liquid starts to boil put a lid on the pan, turn the heat down to minimum and cook for 20 minutes. Do not remove the lid during this time.

While the onion mixture is cooking, skin the chicken breasts, remove any connective tissue and cut the meat into chunks about 25mm square.

When the onion mixture is cooked, take the pan off the heat and remove the lid. Take out the cassia bark and set aside. Now take a potato masher and thoroughly mash the onions, garlic and ginger until you get a fairly smooth purée.

Return the pan to the heat, still at its lowest setting, and add the ground coriander, ground cumin, chilli powder, turmeric, paprika and ground cloves.

Warm through the spices for about 1 minute, stirring all the time to mix them in thoroughly. Return the cassia bark to the pan.

Raise the heat to medium and add the chicken chunks. Stir until the pieces of chicken have turned white over most of their surface.

Add the tomato paste, black pepper, salt and 30ml water. Stir to mix all the ingredients and bring the mixture to a simmer.

Simmer the chicken for 15 minutes (less if you used small chunks).

If the mixture starts getting a little dry add 15ml water – no more just yet. As the chicken is cooking, add more water if the sauce gets too dry but, again, only 15ml at a time. Make sure the sauce is quite thick before you add the butter.

While the chicken is cooking prepare the tomato for the garnish. Cut the tomato into 8 wedges. Melt 5ml butter in a frying pan over a medium heat. When the butter is hot, slide the tomato wedges into the frying pan and fry for about 1 minute on each side. Remove the frying pan from the heat and set aside, leaving the tomato wedges in the pan to keep warm.

About 2 minutes before the chicken is ready add 15ml chopped coriander leaves and 10ml butter. Stir to mix in the coriander leaves and melt the butter. Once the butter has melted add just a little water if the sauce is still too thick. Do not let the sauce boil after you have added the butter or else it will split.

Check that the chicken is thoroughly cooked and remove the piece of cassia bark.

Serve garnished with the fried tomato wedges and a sprinkling of chopped coriander leaves.

Bhuna

The restaurant Bhuna is a well-spiced curry with a thick sauce and medium in heat.

Although the Bhuna is a popular restaurant dish the term *bhuna* is actually a cooking process. In their book Classic Cooking of Punjab the authors Jiggs Kalra, Pushpesh Pant and Raminder Malhotra tell us that the bhuna technique is similar to stir frying where you cook the spices with the onions, garlic and ginger until all the moisture has been driven off. Then the meat is added and you repeat the process until all the meat juices have evaporated. So this dish uses the bhuna method until the sauce has condensed and acquired a deep flavour.

You often get pieces of fried green pepper in the Bhuna in Indian restaurants and I've followed their example. You can leave out the green pepper if you like.

ingredients

45ml vegetable oil
25mm piece of cassia bark
250g onions – finely chopped
2 cloves garlic – finely grated
grated ginger (about half the
    volume of the garlic)
60ml water

350g chicken breast

75g green pepper (trimmed
    weight)
2.5ml vegetable oil to cook the
    green pepper

5ml ground coriander seed

Heat 45ml oil in the heavy-bottomed pan on a medium heat. While the oil is heating up, finely chop the onion.

When the oil is hot, add the cassia bark and stir to coat it in oil. Then add the chopped onion to the pan and stir fry for 5 minutes. The onions should not brown, so lower the heat a little if they start to fry too hard.

While the onions are frying, grate the garlic and ginger onto a small plate but make sure to give the onions a good stir from time to time so they don't start browning.

Spoon the grated garlic and ginger into the pan (plus any juices left on the plate). Stir in well and stir fry continuously for 2 minutes.

5ml ground cumin seed

2.5ml **hot** chilli powder

5ml turmeric

5ml paprika

2 pinches ground cloves

2 pinches ground cardamom
    seeds

5ml tomato paste

2 grinds of black peppercorns

salt to taste

water to loosen the sauce

[optional] 10ml ghee or
    vegetable oil

2 pinches dried fenugreek
    (*kazuri methi*) leaves

kitchen equipment

hand-held food grater with fine
    holes

potato masher

20cm heavy-bottomed pan

small frying pan

Add 60ml water and mix in thoroughly.

Once the liquid starts to boil put a lid on the pan, turn the heat down to minimum and cook for 20 minutes. Do not remove the lid during this time.

While the onion mixture is cooking, skin the chicken breasts, remove any connective tissue and cut the meat into chunks about 25mm square.

Take a green pepper, cut it into quarters lengthways and remove the seeds and pith. Weigh out 75g and refrigerate the rest for another meal. Cut the pepper quarters into chunks about 15mm x 20mm in size. Now heat a small frying pan over a medium heat and add 2.5ml oil. Add the pepper chunks and stir fry until the skins just start to show pale areas. Spoon out the pieces of green pepper onto a plate and set aside.

When the onion mixture is cooked, take the pan off the heat and remove the lid. Remove the cassia bark and set aside. Now take a potato masher and thoroughly mash the onions, garlic and ginger until you get a fairly smooth purée.

Return the pan to the heat, still at its lowest setting, and add the ground coriander, ground cumin, chilli powder, turmeric, paprika, ground cloves and ground cardamom seeds.

Warm through the spices for about 1 minute, stirring all the time to mix them in thoroughly.

Raise the heat to medium and add the chicken chunks. Stir until the pieces of chicken have turned white over most of their surface. Return the cassia bark to the pan.

Add the tomato paste, black pepper, salt and 45ml water. Stir to mix all the ingredients and bring the mixture to a simmer.

Simmer the chicken for 15 minutes (less if you used small chunks).

10 minutes before the end of the cooking time add the fried green pepper chunks to the pan and stir to mix.

If the mixture starts getting a little dry add 15ml water – no more just yet. As the chicken is cooking, add more water if the sauce gets too dry but, again, only 15ml at a time. If you like your curries very rich you could add 10ml ghee or vegetable oil to loosen the curry instead of 10ml water.

5 minutes before the chicken is ready add the dried fenugreek leaves and stir to mix.

Check that the chicken is thoroughly cooked and remove the cassia bark. Serve.

Korma

In Indian restaurants, Chicken Korma is chicken cooked in a mildly spiced, creamy sauce.

Although a korma is mild and lacking in chilli heat it should not be bland. The spicing should be enough to stand out in the sauce, which is enriched with ground almonds and coconut cream. Korma is often recommended as the dish to offer diners who are new to Indian restaurants but it is still extremely popular with people who like their curries mild and creamy.

The restaurant korma tends to be the basis for other milder curries on the menu which contain fruit of some kind: sultanas, pineapple, lychees, etc. If you fancy making one of those curries, use the korma as a base and add your chosen fruit near the end of the cooking to warm through.

ingredients

30ml vegetable oil
150g onions – finely chopped
2 cloves garlic – finely grated
grated ginger (about the same
   the volume as the garlic)
45ml water

350g chicken breast
30ml ground almonds

5ml ground coriander seed
2.5ml ground cumin seed
¼ of a 2.5ml spoon *hot* chilli
   powder
⅓ of a 2.5ml spoon turmeric
2 pinches ground cloves
2 pinches ground cardamom
   seeds

Heat 30ml oil in the heavy-bottomed pan on a medium heat. While the oil is heating up, finely chop the onion.

When the oil is hot add the chopped onions and stir fry for 5 minutes. The onions should not brown, so lower the heat a little if they start to fry too hard.

While the onions are frying, grate the garlic and ginger onto a small plate but make sure to give the onions a good stir from time to time so they don't start browning.

Spoon the grated garlic and ginger into the pan (plus any juices left on the plate). Stir in well and stir fry continuously for 2 minutes.

Add 45ml water and mix in thoroughly.

Once the liquid starts to boil put a lid on the pan, turn the heat down to minimum and cook for 20 minutes. Do not remove the lid during this time.

1 pinch ground mace

25g creamed coconut – chopped
    into chunks
2 grinds of black peppercorns
salt to taste

water to loosen the sauce
30ml double cream (at room
    temperature)

kitchen equipment

hand-held food grater with fine
    holes
potato masher
20cm heavy-bottomed pan

While the onion mixture is cooking, skin the chicken breasts, remove any connective tissue and cut the meat into chunks about 25mm square.

When the onion mixture is cooked, take the pan off the heat and remove the lid. Take a potato masher and thoroughly mash the onions, garlic and ginger until you get a fairly smooth purée.

Return the pan to the heat and add the ground almonds. Raise the heat a little to get things sizzling then turn the heat back to low and stir fry for 2 minutes.

Add the ground coriander, ground cumin, chilli powder, turmeric, ground cloves, ground cardamom seeds and ground mace.

Stir to mix and warm through the spices for about 1 minute.

Raise the heat to medium and add the chicken chunks. Stir until the pieces of chicken have turned white over most of their surface.

Add the creamed coconut, black pepper, salt and 60ml water. Stir the ingredients until the creamed coconut has melted and then bring the mixture to a simmer.

Simmer the chicken for 15minutes (less if you used small chunks).

If the mixture starts getting a little dry add 15ml water – you probably won't need more than that.

2 minutes before the chicken is ready make sure the sauce is fairly thick and then add the double cream. Stir to mix and gently warm the sauce without boiling or the cream will split.

Check that the chicken is thoroughly cooked. Serve.

Madras

The Madras and the Chicken Tikka Masala were invented by British Bangladeshi chefs to cater for the tastes of their non-Asian customers. They share the honour of being the best-selling curries over time, not only in Indian restaurants (most of which are run by Bangladeshis despite their name) but also in supermarket ready meals.

The city of Madras, now known as Chennai, was the centre for blending curry powder in the days of the British Raj in India. Madras curry powder was exported to the UK and all around the British Empire so that the British could make curries even though they may have lacked the essential fresh ingredients. It seems fair to assume that, when the pioneers of High Street Indian restaurants in the 1960s wanted to introduce a standard hot curry for their restaurant menu, calling it Madras would make it easily recognisable to the average Brit, and the name has been in use ever since.

Not only is the Madras curry still extremely popular but "Madras hot" has become the *lingua franca* in UK curry houses to describe a curry which is most definitely hot but not so hot that it makes your mouth explode and your body sweat uncontrollably. Yet, because the Madras is a restaurant invention, there is no traditional recipe to fall back on, which explains why there can be such a variation in the Madras from restaurant to restaurant.

ingredients

45ml vegetable oil
1 bay leaf
250g onions – finely chopped
2 cloves garlic – finely grated
grated ginger (about half the
   volume of the garlic)
60ml water

350g chicken breast

Heat 45ml oil in the heavy-bottomed pan on a medium heat. While the oil is heating up, finely chop the onion.

When the oil is hot, add the bay leaf and stir to coat it in oil. Then add the chopped onion to the pan and stir fry for 5 minutes. The onions should not brown, so lower the heat a little if they start to fry too hard.

While the onions are frying, grate the garlic and ginger onto a small plate but make sure to give the

5ml ground coriander seed

5ml ground cumin seed

5ml **hot** chilli powder

2.5ml turmeric

5ml paprika

3 pinches ground cloves

2 pinches ground mace (or
    nutmeg)

5ml lemon juice

20ml tomato paste

3 grinds of black peppercorns

salt to taste

water to loosen the sauce

[optional] 10ml ghee or
    vegetable oil

2 pinches dried fenugreek
    (*kasuri methi*) leaves

kitchen equipment

hand-held food grater with fine
    holes

potato masher

20cm heavy-bottomed pan

onions a good stir from time to time so they don't start browning.

Spoon the grated garlic and ginger into the pan (plus any juices left on the plate). Stir in well and stir fry continuously for 2 minutes.

Add 60ml water and mix in thoroughly.

Once the liquid starts to boil put a lid on the pan, turn the heat down to minimum and cook for 20 minutes. Do not remove the lid during this time.

While the onion mixture is cooking, skin the chicken breasts, remove any connective tissue and cut the meat into chunks about 25mm square.

When the onion mixture is cooked, take the pan off the heat and remove the lid. Remove the bay leaf and set aside. Now take a potato masher and thoroughly mash the onions, garlic and ginger until you get a fairly smooth purée.

Return the pan to the heat, still at its lowest setting, and add the ground coriander, ground cumin, chilli powder, turmeric, paprika, ground cloves and ground mace.

Warm through the spices for about 1 minute, stirring all the time to mix them in thoroughly.

Raise the heat to medium and add the chicken chunks. Stir until the pieces of chicken have turned white over most of their surface. Return the bay leaf to the pan.

Add the lemon juice, tomato paste, black pepper, salt and 30ml water. Stir to mix all the ingredients and bring the mixture to a simmer.

Simmer the chicken for 15 minutes (less if you used small chunks).

If the mixture starts getting a little dry add 15ml water – no more just yet. As the chicken is cooking, add more water if the sauce gets too dry but, again, only 15ml at a time. If you like your curries very rich you could add 10ml ghee or vegetable oil to loosen the curry instead of 10ml water.

5 minutes before the chicken is ready add the dried fenugreek leaves and stir to mix.

Check that the chicken is thoroughly cooked and remove the bay leaf. Serve.

Pasanda

Chicken Pasanda is a popular Indian restaurant curry but, in traditional recipes, pasanda is not a curry at all nor is it made with chicken.

Pasanda are kebabs of thinly sliced fillets of marinated lamb. The lamb fillets are threaded onto broad-bladed skewers and barbecued over charcoal. Badam (almond) Pasanda is made by spreading a spicy almond paste over the lamb fillets and then rolling them. The lamb rolls are then fried before finally being cooked a creamy sauce.

The restaurant pasanda does away with stuffing and rolling the meat but instead incorporates the ground almonds into the sauce. A pasanda is well spiced for a creamy curry, although it is usually served mild to medium. Chicken Pasanda is usually served garnished with toasted, flaked almonds.

ingredients

30ml vegetable oil
20mm piece of cassia bark
150g onions – finely chopped
2 cloves garlic – finely grated
grated ginger (about the same
   the volume as the garlic)
45ml water

350g chicken breast
flaked almonds (enough for the
   garnish)
45ml ground almonds

5ml ground coriander seed
2.5ml ground cumin seed
⅓ of a 2.5ml spoon *hot* chilli
   powder
½ a 2.5ml spoon turmeric

Heat 30ml oil in the heavy-bottomed pan on a medium heat. While the oil is heating up, finely chop the onion.

When the oil is hot, add the piece of cassia bark and stir to coat it in oil. Then add the chopped onions and stir fry for 5 minutes. The onions should not brown, so lower the heat a little if they start to fry too hard.

While the onions are frying, grate the garlic and ginger onto a small plate but make sure to give the onions a good stir from time to time so they don't start browning.

Spoon the grated garlic and ginger into the pan (plus any juices left on the plate). Stir in well and stir fry continuously for 2 minutes.

Add 45ml water and mix in thoroughly.

Once the liquid starts to boil put a lid on the pan, turn the heat down to minimum and cook for 20 minutes.

3 pinches ground mace (or
    ground nutmeg)
2 pinches ground cardamom
    seeds

15ml tomato paste
2 pinches sugar
2 grinds of black peppercorns
salt to taste

water to loosen the sauce
30ml double cream (at room
    temperature)

kitchen equipment

hand-held food grater with fine
    holes
potato masher
20cm heavy-bottomed pan
small frying pan

Do not remove the lid during this time.

While the onion mixture is cooking, skin the chicken breasts, remove any connective tissue and cut the meat into chunks about 25mm square.

Heat a small frying pan on a medium/low heat and add the flaked almonds. Heat the almonds, stirring and flipping them over from time to time, until nice brown patches start to appear on both sides. Slide the toasted almonds out of the frying pan onto a plate. Set aside.

When the onion mixture is cooked, take the pan off the heat and remove the lid. Remove the cassia bark and set aside. Now take a potato masher and thoroughly mash the onions, garlic and ginger until you get a fairly smooth purée.

Return the pan to the heat and add the ground almonds. Raise the heat a little to get things sizzling then turn the heat back to low and stir fry for 2 minutes.

Add the ground coriander, ground cumin, chilli powder, turmeric, ground mace and ground cardamom seeds.

Warm through the spices for about 1 minute, stirring all the time to mix them in thoroughly. Return the cassia bark to the pan.

Raise the heat to medium and add the chicken chunks. Stir until the pieces of chicken have turned white over most of their surface.

Add the tomato paste, sugar, black pepper, salt and 60ml water. Stir to mix all the ingredients and bring the mixture to a simmer.

Simmer the chicken for 15 minutes (less if you used small chunks).

If the mixture starts getting a little dry add 15ml water – no more just yet. As the chicken is cooking, add more water if the sauce gets too dry but, again, only 15ml at a time.

2 minutes before the chicken is ready make sure the sauce is quite thick then add the double cream. Stir to mix and gently warm the sauce without bringing it back to a simmer. If the sauce is still too thick add a little more water.

Check that the chicken is thoroughly cooked and remove the cassia bark from the pan.

Serve garnished with the toasted almonds.

Dopiaza

I love Chicken Dopiaza but regrettably it isn't often made in the old-fashioned curry house way in many restaurants these days. My recipe doesn't go back to the days when the dopiaza was served with great chunks of fried onion and pieces of boiled chicken swimming in a sauce topped by a pool of ghee but it does have lots more flavour and more character than some restaurant versions I've tried recently.

The dopiaza was a top seller in the British curry houses of the 1970s but the British enjoyed their dopiaza long before that. In 1618 an English chaplain in India called Edward Terry was entertained at the court of the Moghul emperor Jahangir and wrote that the dopiaza he had been served was "the most savoury meat I ever tasted".

Dopiaza means double onions. Some traditional recipes take that as meaning that the onions should be double the weight of the meat in the recipe. Mrs Balbir Singh, in her classic book Indian Cookery, disagrees and says that the onion should be equal to the weight of the meat and should be incorporated into the dish "in two different ways, half of it being added in the fried state and the other half in the raw".

Chicken Dopiaza is strong tasting but only medium in heat.

ingredients

45ml vegetable oil
25mm piece cassia bark
2 pinches black cumin seeds
250g onions – finely chopped
2 cloves garlic – finely grated
grated ginger (about half the
  volume of the garlic)
60ml water

350g chicken breast

Heat 45ml oil in the heavy-bottomed pan on a medium heat. While the oil is heating up, finely chop 250g of onion.

When the oil is hot, add the cassia bark and black cumin seeds and stir to coat them in oil. Then add the chopped onion to the pan and stir fry for 5 minutes. The onions should not brown, so lower the heat a little if they start to fry too hard.

While the onions are frying, grate the garlic and ginger onto a small plate but make sure to give the

100g onions – cut into chunks
    as per method
5ml vegetable oil to cook the
    onion chunks

7.5ml ground coriander seed
7.5ml ground cumin seed
2.5 ml *hot* chilli powder
5ml turmeric
2 pinches ground cloves
2 pinches ground cardamom
    seeds

2.5ml lemon juice
5ml tomato paste
2 grinds of black peppercorns
salt to taste

water to loosen the sauce
[optional] 10ml ghee or
    vegetable oil

2 pinches dried fenugreek
    (*kazuri methi*) leaves

kitchen equipment

hand-held food grater with fine
    holes
potato masher
20cm heavy-bottomed pan
karahi or wok

onions a good stir from time to time so they don't start browning.

Spoon the grated garlic and ginger into the pan (plus any juices left on the plate). Stir in well and stir fry continuously for 2 minutes.

Add 60ml water and mix in thoroughly.

Once the liquid starts to boil put a lid on the pan, turn the heat down to minimum and cook for 20 minutes. Do not remove the lid during this time.

While the onion mixture is cooking, skin the chicken breasts, remove any connective tissue and cut the meat into chunks about 25mm square.

Take the second lot of onions (100g) and cut into large chunks about 20mm across.

Heat a karahi containing 5ml oil on a high heat. When the oil is hot, slide in the chunks of onion and stir fry until the onion pieces are brown all around the edges (about 3 minutes). Spoon the onion pieces onto a plate and set aside.

When the onion mixture is cooked, take the pan off the heat and remove the lid. Take out the cassia bark and set aside. Now take a potato masher and thoroughly mash the onions, garlic and ginger until you get a fairly smooth purée.

Return the pan to the heat, still at its lowest setting, and add the ground coriander, ground cumin, chilli powder, turmeric, ground cloves and ground cardamom seeds.

Warm through the spices for about 1 minute, stirring all the time to mix them in thoroughly. Return the cassia bark to the pan.

Raise the heat to medium and add the chicken chunks. Stir until the pieces of chicken have turned white over most of their surface.

Add the lemon juice, tomato paste, black pepper, salt and 45ml water. Stir to mix all the ingredients and bring the mixture to a simmer.

Simmer the chicken for 15 minutes (less if you used small chunks).

10 minutes before the end of the cooking add the reserved chunks of fried onion and stir to mix.

If the mixture starts getting a little dry add 15ml water – no more just yet. As the chicken is cooking, add more water if the sauce gets too dry but, again, only 15ml at a time. If you like your curries very rich you could add 10ml ghee or vegetable oil to loosen the curry instead of 10ml water.

5 minutes before the chicken is ready add the dried fenugreek leaves and stir to mix.

Check that the chicken is thoroughly cooked and remove the cassia bark. Serve.

Jalfrezi

Chicken Jalfrezi in Indian restaurants has traditionally been cooked using fresh green chillies. The supermarket version of the jalfrezi often dispenses with the fresh chillies and uses red or green peppers instead. I have noticed that quite a few restaurants have started using a combination of chillies and peppers so that the dish is now more like the restaurant Korai but with added chillies. Whatever the style, the jalfrezi is one of the hotter dishes on the restaurant menu.

The number of chillies you use depends on how hot you like your jalfrezi and how hot the chillies are. Fresh chillies are notoriously variable in their heat, so take a little nibble of one of the thin green chillies and make a judgement on how many to use. Taste your jalfrezi about 5 minutes before the end of the cooking. If you find you've underestimated how many chillies you needed you can always add a pinch of two of hot chilli powder to liven things up a bit.

ingredients

45ml vegetable oil
200g onions – finely chopped
1 dried bay leaf
2 cloves garlic – finely grated
grated ginger (about the same
    volume as the garlic)
45ml water

350g chicken breast
½ a medium onion (about 75g
    trimmed weight) – sliced as in
    method
5ml vegetable oil to fry the
    onion strips
4 – 8 thin green chillies

Heat 45ml oil in the heavy-bottomed pan on a medium heat. While the oil is heating up, finely chop the onion.

When the oil is hot, add the bay leaf and stir it around to coat it in oil. Then add the chopped onions and stir fry for 5 minutes. The onions should not brown, so lower the heat a little if they start to fry too hard.

While the onions are frying, grate the garlic and ginger onto a small plate but make sure to give the onions a good stir from time to time so they don't start browning.

Spoon the grated garlic and ginger into the pan (plus any juices left on the plate). Stir in well and stir fry continuously for 2 minutes.

5ml ground coriander seed

5ml ground cumin seed

2.5ml turmeric

3 pinches ground cloves

2 pinches ground cardamom
seeds

10ml tomato paste

2.5ml lemon juice

2 grinds of black peppercorns

salt to taste

water to loosen the sauce

10ml finely chopped coriander
leaves

kitchen equipment

hand-held food grater with fine
holes

potato masher

20cm heavy-bottomed pan

karahi or wok

Add 45ml water and mix in thoroughly.

Once the liquid starts to boil put a lid on the pan, turn the heat down to minimum and cook for 20 minutes. Do not remove the lid during this time.

While the onion mixture is cooking, skin the chicken breasts, remove any connective tissue and cut the meat into chunks about 25mm square.

Place the onion half, cut-side down, on a chopping board and cut it into slices about 3-4mm across. Then cut the slices in half crossways so you get lots of short strips.

Heat a karahi over a medium-high heat and add 5ml oil. Slide the onion strips into the hot pan. Now stir fry the onion strips until they turn a fairly even brown colour but before the edges start to burn. Spoon out the onion strips onto a plate and set aside.

Slice the stalks off the chillies and cut them in half lengthways. Remove the seeds and pith by sliding a teaspoon along the length of the chilli half. Set aside.

When the onion mixture is cooked, take the pan off the heat and remove the lid. Take out the bay leaf and set aside. Now take a potato masher and thoroughly mash the onions, garlic and ginger until you get a fairly smooth purée.

Return the pan to the heat, still at its lowest setting, and add the ground coriander, ground cumin, turmeric, ground cloves and ground cardamom seeds.

Warm through the spices for about 1 minute, stirring all the time to mix them in thoroughly.

Raise the heat to medium and add the chicken chunks. Stir until the pieces of chicken have turned white over most of their surface. Return the bay leaf to the pan.

Add the tomato paste, lemon juice, black pepper, salt and 15ml water. Stir to mix all the ingredients and bring the mixture to a simmer.

Simmer the chicken for 15 minutes (less if you used small chunks).

If the mixture starts getting a little dry add 15ml water – no more just yet. As the chicken is cooking, add more water if the sauce gets too dry but, again, only 15ml at a time.

10 minutes before the end of the cooking add the chilli halves and the reserved strips of fried onion. Stir to mix and gently poke the chilli halves down into the liquid so they cook right through and spread their heat into the sauce.

2 minutes before the chicken is ready add the finely chopped coriander leaves and stir to mix.

Check that the chicken is thoroughly cooked. Remove the bay leaf and serve.

Tikka Masala

In order to cook this recipe within 1 hour from start to finish it is not possible to use marinated and cooked chicken tikka, so we need to use plain chicken instead.

Chicken Tikka Masala, like the Madras, is the creation of British Bangladeshi chefs to suit the tastes of their non-Asian customers. But, however inauthentic it may be, Chicken Tikka Masala still outsells every other curry when you consider the total sold both in restaurants and as supermarket ready meals. Because Chicken Tikka Masala is a restaurant invention there is no traditional recipe on which to base the dish. That explains why there can be such a variation in the dish from one restaurant (and one supermarket) to another.

You will find that the recipe uses less than half of the cashew nut purée but I don't recommend making a smaller amount. My cooking tests showed that the measures used are the minimum needed to obtain a smooth purée in a small blender. The good news is that it freezes well so you can make a full portion and save the rest for the next time you make the recipe or use it to make Shahi Chicken in the House Specials chapter.

ingredients

30ml vegetable oil
150g onions – finely chopped
2 cloves garlic – finely grated
grated ginger (about the same
  the volume as the garlic)
45ml water

350g chicken breast
50g unsalted, raw cashew nuts

5ml ground coriander seed

Heat 30ml oil in the heavy-bottomed pan on a medium heat. While the oil is heating up, finely chop the onion.

When the oil is hot, add the chopped onions and stir fry for 5 minutes. The onions should not brown, so lower the heat a little if they start to fry too hard.

While the onions are frying, grate the garlic and ginger onto a small plate but make sure to give the onions a good stir from time to time so they don't start browning.

Spoon the grated garlic and ginger into the pan (plus

2.5ml ground cumin seed

⅔ a 2.5ml spoon turmeric

⅓ of a 2.5ml spoon **hot** chilli powder

2 pinches ground cloves

2 pinches ground cardamom seeds

1 pinch ground cinnamon

30ml Greek-style full fat yoghurt

5ml syrup from a jar of mango chutney or 5ml smooth mango chutney

20ml tomato paste

2 grinds of black peppercorns

salt to taste

water to loosen the sauce

kitchen equipment

hand-held food grater with fine holes

potato masher

20cm heavy-bottomed pan

small-capacity food blender – a baby food blender is ideal

rubber spatula

any juices left on the plate). Stir in well and stir fry continuously for 2 minutes.

Add 45ml water and mix in thoroughly.

Once the liquid starts to boil put a lid on the pan, turn the heat down to minimum and cook for 20 minutes. Do not remove the lid during this time.

While the onion mixture is cooking, skin the chicken breasts, remove any connective tissue and cut the meat into chunks about 25mm square.

Now make the cashew nut purée. Dry roast the cashew nuts on a medium/low heat until they are covered in nice brown patches. Let the roasted cashew nuts cool a little and then place them in a small blender together with 75ml water. Blend well until very smooth. Pour out the cashew nut purée into a small bowl and scrape round the blender with a rubber spatula to get all the remaining purée out of the blender. Set aside.

When the onion mixture is cooked, take the pan off the heat and remove the lid. Take a potato masher and thoroughly mash the onions, garlic and ginger until you get a fairly smooth purée.

Return the pan to the heat, still at its lowest setting, and add the ground coriander, ground cumin, turmeric, chilli powder, ground cloves, ground cardamom seeds and ground cinnamon.

Stir to mix and warm through the spices for about 1 minute, stirring all the time.

Raise the heat to medium and add the chicken chunks. Stir until the pieces of chicken have turned white over most of their surface.

Spoon the yoghurt into the pan and stir to mix. Be careful not to overheat the yoghurt or it will split.

Add the mango chutney syrup, tomato paste, black pepper, salt, only 30ml of the cashew nut purée and 30ml water. Stir the ingredients to mix thoroughly.

Simmer the chicken for 15 minutes (less if you used small chunks).

If the mixture starts getting a little dry add 15ml water – no more just yet. As the chicken is cooking, add more water if the sauce gets too dry but, again, only 15ml at a time.

Check that the chicken is thoroughly cooked. Serve.

Saag

Most restaurants offer a dish called Saag in which chicken, lamb or prawns are cooked in a medium sauce with chopped spinach. *Saag* is a general term for numerous green leaves used in cooking, such as fresh fenugreek leaves, spinach leaves and other green leaves. Sometimes you will see this dish on a restaurant menu described as Chicken Palak. It is the same dish but *palak* is the name for spinach alone.

My recipe uses frozen baby leaf spinach rather than fresh leaves because the texture more closely resembles the restaurant version and using frozen spinach is very convenient. You can use fresh spinach leaves if you like but you will need to cook them until tender, drain off the liquid and then weigh out the required amount.

ingredients

120g frozen baby spinach leaves
  – thawed and drained of water

45ml vegetable oil
25mm piece of cassia bark
200g onions – finely chopped
2 cloves garlic – finely grated
grated ginger (about the same
  volume as the garlic)
45ml water

350g chicken breast
1 clove garlic – sliced as in
  method
2.5ml vegetable oil to fry the
  garlic slices

5ml ground coriander seed

Thaw 120g frozen baby spinach leaves in a sieve over a bowl. You need 100g once the spinach has thawed and separated from its watery coating. Discard the liquid.

Heat 45ml oil in the heavy-bottomed pan on a medium heat. While the oil is heating up, finely chop the onion.

When the oil is hot, add the cassia bark and stir to coat it in oil. Then add the chopped onion to the pan and stir fry for 5 minutes. The onions should not brown, so lower the heat a little if they start to fry too hard.

While the onions are frying, grate the garlic and ginger onto a small plate but make sure to give the onions a good stir from time to time so they don't start browning.

Spoon the grated garlic and ginger into the pan (plus any juices left on the plate). Stir in well and stir fry

7.5ml ground cumin seed

2.5ml **hot** chilli powder

2.5ml turmeric

3 pinches ground mace (or
nutmeg)

2.5ml lemon juice

2 grinds of black peppercorns

salt to taste

water to loosen the sauce

2 pinches dried fenugreek
(*kasuri methi*) leaves

15ml butter cut into small
chunks

kitchen equipment

hand-held food grater with fine
holes
potato masher
20cm heavy-bottomed pan
small frying pan

continuously for 2 minutes.

Add 45ml water and mix in thoroughly.

Once the liquid starts to boil put a lid on the pan, turn the heat down to minimum and cook for 20 minutes. Do not remove the lid during this time.

While the onion mixture is cooking, skin the chicken breasts, remove any connective tissue and cut the meat into chunks about 25mm square.

Trim and peel a clove of garlic. Cut the garlic crossways into thin slices and then cut each slice into strips about 2mm wide.

Heat 2.5ml oil in a small frying pan over a medium heat.

Slide the garlic slices into the pan and fry, stirring continuously, until the garlic is just turning brown and is giving off a smoky aroma. Now quickly remove the fried garlic slices from the pan onto a cold plate. Set aside.

When the onion mixture is cooked, take the pan off the heat and remove the lid. Remove the cassia bark and set aside. Now take a potato masher and thoroughly mash the onions, garlic and ginger until you get a fairly smooth purée.

Return the pan to the heat, still at its lowest setting, and add the ground coriander, ground cumin, chilli powder, turmeric and ground mace.

Warm through the spices for about 1 minute, stirring all the time to mix them in thoroughly.

Raise the heat to medium and add the chicken chunks. Stir until the pieces of chicken have turned white over most of their surface. Return the cassia bark to the pan.

Add the reserved fried garlic slices, lemon juice, black

pepper, salt and 30ml water. Stir to mix all the ingredients and bring the mixture to a simmer.

Simmer the chicken for 15 minutes (less if you used small chunks).

If the mixture starts getting a little dry add 15ml water – no more just yet. As the chicken is cooking, add more water if the sauce gets too dry but, again, only 15ml at a time. Make sure the sauce is quite thick before you add the spinach and the butter. The spinach will drop water and the melted butter will also loosen the sauce.

5 minutes before the chicken is ready, add the dried fenugreek leaves and the thawed spinach and stir to mix.

1 minute before the end of the cooking add 15ml butter and stir to melt the butter and mix it into the sauce. Do not bring the sauce back to a simmer or the butter may split.

Check that the chicken is thoroughly cooked and remove the cassia bark. Serve.

Dhansak

Dhansak is **the** signature Parsee dish.

The Parsee chef Cyrus Todiwala tells us in his book, Café Spice Namaste, that an authentic dhansak contains aubergines and other vegetables and many different types of dhal (the "sak" in the name). It is made with lamb and accompanied by a *cachumber*, which is an onion, tomato and herb salad. The "dhan" part of the name means rice and a dhansak is traditionally served with a *pulao* of fried and spiced rice.

The regular Indian restaurant dhansak is much simpler than the authentic Parsee dish. It is basically chicken, lamb or prawns in a hot, sweet and sour sauce with lentils. Despite Cyrus Todiwala's criticism that the dhansak has been "grossly abused" by restaurants, my recipe follows the curry house style rather than the authentic Parsee version.

The dhansak recipe in my previous book uses chana dhal but, much as I enjoy it, I have not used this relative of the chick pea in the recipe. The reason is that chana dhal needs soaking for some hours before use and that would not be compatible with cooking the whole curry within an hour, so I have used only red lentils but with very good results. If you have plenty of time you could use a mixture of half chana dhal and half red lentils, which will give a more authentic texture.

The amount of red lentils (30ml when dry) might seem far too little but the lentils absorb their own volume of water while cooking and you'll end up with just the right amount for a balanced dish. After all, the dish is chicken with lentils and not lentils with chicken.

ingredients

30ml split red lentils (masoor
  dhal)
10ml butter
350ml water (to cook the lentils;
  not to be added to the sauce)

Start by cooking the lentils. Measure out 30ml red lentils and pour them into a measuring jug. Now place the jug under running cold water and wash the lentils. Once the jug is full, let the lentils settle and then pour out most of the water, without losing any lentils. Repeat the washing process 4 or 5 times. Finally,

45ml vegetable oil

3 "petals" from a whole star
anise

25mm piece cassia bark

200g onions – finely chopped

2 cloves garlic – finely grated

grated ginger (about the same
the volume as the garlic)

45ml water

350g chicken breast

7.5ml ground coriander seed

7.5ml ground cumin seed

¾ of a 5ml spoon **hot** chilli
powder

2.5ml turmeric

3 pinches ground cloves

3 pinches ground cardamom
seeds

10ml lemon juice

¾ of a 5ml spoon sugar

10ml tomato paste

2 grinds of black peppercorns

salt to taste (use a little more
than other curries as the
lentils are quite bland)

water to loosen the sauce

[optional] 10ml butter

2 pinches dried fenugreek
(*kasuri methi*) leaves

drain the lentils into a sieve.

Transfer the washed lentils into a saucepan (about 18cm diameter) containing 350ml cold water. Add 10ml butter and bring the water to the boil.

Boil the lentils vigorously for 5 minutes and then turn the heat down to a simmer. Do not cover the pan. Simmer the lentils until virtually all the water has evaporated or been absorbed by the lentils. Be careful in the final stages of the cooking that you don't use up all the water and start to burn the lentils on the bottom of the pan.

While the lentils are cooking, heat 45ml oil in the heavy-bottomed pan on a medium heat and finely chop the onion.

When the oil is hot, add the pieces of star anise and cassia bark and stir to coat them in oil. Then add the chopped onions and stir fry for 5 minutes. The onions should not brown, so lower the heat a little if they start to fry too hard.

While the onions are frying, grate the garlic and ginger onto a small plate but make sure to give the onions a good stir from time to time so they don't start browning.

Spoon the grated garlic and ginger into the pan (plus any juices left on the plate). Stir in well and stir fry continuously for 2 minutes.

Add 45ml water and mix in thoroughly.

Once the liquid starts to boil put a lid on the pan, turn the heat down to minimum and cook for 20 minutes. Do not remove the lid during this time.

When the lentils are cooked take the pan off the heat, put a lid on it and set aside.

kitchen equipment

18cm saucepan
hand-held food grater with fine
  holes
potato masher
20cm heavy-bottomed pan

While the onion mixture is cooking, skin the chicken breasts, remove any connective tissue and cut the meat into chunks about 25mm square.

When the onion mixture is cooked, take the pan off the heat and remove the lid. Take out the star anise and cassia bark and set aside. Now take a potato masher and thoroughly mash the onions, garlic and ginger until you get a fairly smooth purée.

Return the pan to the heat, still at its lowest setting, and add the ground coriander, ground cumin, chilli powder, turmeric, ground cloves and the ground cardamom seeds.

Warm through the spices for about 1 minute, stirring all the time to mix them in thoroughly. Return the star anise and cassia bark to the pan.

Raise the heat to medium and add the chicken chunks. Stir until the pieces of chicken have turned white over most of their surface.

Add the lemon juice, sugar, tomato paste, black pepper, salt, the reserved lentils along with any liquid left in the pan and 30-45ml water (depending how much lentil liquid you've got). Stir to mix all the ingredients and bring the mixture to a simmer.

Simmer the chicken for 15 minutes (less if you used small chunks).

If the mixture starts getting a little dry add 15ml water – no more just yet. As the chicken is cooking, add more water if the sauce gets too dry but, again, only 15ml at a time. If you like your curries rich (I do) you can add 10ml butter to loosen the curry instead of 10ml water.

Taste the sauce and adjust the sweet/sour balance to your liking by adding more sugar or more lemon juice.

5 minutes before the chicken is ready add the dried fenugreek leaves and stir to mix.

Check that the chicken is thoroughly cooked. Remove the pieces of star anise and the cassia bark and discard. Serve the dhansak.

Patia

Patia is a traditional Parsee dish made with fish cooked in a dark vinegar sauce.

The restaurant patia tends not to have much in common with the authentic version and is served as chicken, lamb or prawns cooked in a hot, sweet and sour sauce. Some restaurants use lemon juice as the souring agent and others use tamarind paste. I prefer the latter which gives a deeper flavour and a darker colour to the dish.

Chicken Patia is a very popular restaurant dish and my recipe follows the restaurant style rather than the Parsee original. Omit the tomato wedges if you like but I think they round off the curry nicely. If you do omit the tomato wedges then add a little butter to the Patia just before serving.

ingredients

45ml vegetable oil

1 black cardamom pod

3 "petals" from a whole star anise

200g onions – finely chopped

2 cloves garlic – finely grated

grated ginger (about equal the volume of the garlic)

45ml water

350g chicken breast

5ml ground coriander seed

5ml ground cumin seed

⅔ of a 5ml spoon **hot** chilli powder

½ a 2.5ml spoon turmeric

5ml paprika

Heat 45ml oil in the heavy-bottomed pan on a medium heat. While the oil is heating up, finely chop the onion.

When the oil is hot, add the black cardamom pod and the star anise and stir to coat them in oil. Then add the chopped onions and stir fry for 5 minutes. The onions should not brown, so lower the heat a little if they start to fry too hard.

While the onions are frying, grate the garlic and ginger onto a small plate but make sure to give the onions a good stir from time to time so they don't start browning.

Spoon the grated garlic and ginger into the pan (plus any juices left on the plate). Stir in well and stir fry continuously for 2 minutes.

Add 45ml water and mix in thoroughly.

Once the liquid starts to boil put a lid on the pan, turn

20ml tamarind paste

15ml tomato paste

2.5ml sugar

2 grinds of black peppercorns

salt to taste (be careful as the
  tamarind paste will contain
  salt)

water to loosen the sauce

1 good-sized tomato

5ml butter to fry the tomato

finely chopped coriander leaves
  to garnish

kitchen equipment

hand-held food grater with fine
  holes

potato masher

20cm heavy-bottomed pan

frying pan

the heat down to minimum and cook for 20 minutes. Do not remove the lid during this time.

While the onion mixture is cooking, skin the chicken breasts, remove any connective tissue and cut the meat into chunks about 25mm square.

When the onion mixture is cooked, take the pan off the heat and remove the lid. Remove the star anise and the black cardamom pod from the pan and set aside. Now take a potato masher and thoroughly mash the onions, garlic and ginger until you get a fairly smooth purée.

Return the pan to the heat, still at its lowest setting, and add the ground coriander, ground cumin, chilli powder, turmeric and paprika.

Warm through the spices for about 1 minute, stirring all the time to mix them in thoroughly. Return the star anise and the black cardamom pod to the pan.

Raise the heat to medium and add the chicken chunks. Stir until the pieces of chicken have turned white over most of their surface.

Add the tamarind paste, tomato paste, sugar, black pepper, salt and 30ml water. Stir to mix all the ingredients and bring the mixture to a simmer.

Simmer the chicken for 15 minutes (less if you used small chunks).

If the mixture starts getting a little dry add 15ml water. As the chicken is cooking, add more water if the sauce gets too dry but, again, only 15ml at a time.

While the chicken is cooking prepare the tomato for the garnish. Cut the tomato into 8 wedges. Melt 5ml butter in a frying pan over a medium heat. When the butter is hot, slide the tomato wedges into the frying pan and fry for about 1 minute on each side. Remove the frying pan from the heat and set aside, leaving the tomato wedges in the pan to keep warm.

Towards the end of the cooking, taste the curry and adjust the sweet/sour balance if you think it's not quite right by adding a little more tamarind paste or a little more sugar.

Check that the chicken is thoroughly cooked. Remove the black cardamom pod and the pieces of star anise and discard.

Serve garnished with the fried tomato wedges and finely chopped coriander leaves.

Vindaloo

The vindaloo was originally a Portuguese dish which took its name from the two main ingredients, which were "vinho" (wine/wine vinegar) and "alhos" (garlic). Goa, in southern India, was once a Portuguese colony and the locals adapted the Portuguese original by adding chillies – lots of chillies – so it became hot and sour.

The restaurant vindaloo, however, is a world away from the Goan speciality and the only similarity is that it is very, very hot. In some restaurants the vindaloo is the same recipe as the Madras but with added chilli powder. Other restaurants add chunks of potato (a misinterpretation of the "aloo" part of the name to mean potato, as it does for other dishes on the restaurant menu) to their vindaloo. What all vindaloos have in common is that they are searingly hot.

My recipe omits the potato but has a rich, hot sauce enhanced with dried red chillies. The bird eye chillies are small (about 25mm long) but don't be fooled by their size; small definitely does not mean mild. They are volcanically hot but they do give an added dimension to the flavour of the vindaloo. Eat responsibly!

ingredients

45ml vegetable oil
6 dried red bird eye chillies
25mm piece of cassia bark
250g onions – finely chopped
3 cloves garlic – finely grated
grated ginger (about half the
    volume of the garlic)
60ml water

350g chicken breast

Heat 45ml oil in the heavy-bottomed pan on a medium heat. While the oil is heating up, finely chop the onion.

When the oil is hot, add the dried chillies and the cassia bark and stir to coat them in oil. Heat the spices until the chillies start to darken a little. Then add the chopped onion to the pan and stir fry for 5 minutes. The onions should not brown, so lower the heat a little if they start to fry too hard.

While the onions are frying, grate the garlic and ginger onto a small plate but make sure to give the

7.5ml ground coriander seed

5ml ground cumin seed

5ml *hot* chilli powder (add more
   if you like but this is my limit)

2.5ml turmeric

2 pinches ground cloves

5ml red wine vinegar

20ml tomato paste

3 grinds of black peppercorns

salt to taste

water to loosen the sauce

[optional] 10ml ghee or
   vegetable oil

kitchen equipment

hand-held food grater with fine
   holes

potato masher

20cm heavy-bottomed pan

onions a good stir from time to time so they don't start browning.

Spoon the grated garlic and ginger into the pan (plus any juices left on the plate). Stir in well and stir fry continuously for 2 minutes.

Add 60ml water and mix in thoroughly.

Once the liquid starts to boil put a lid on the pan, turn the heat down to minimum and cook for 20 minutes. Do not remove the lid during this time.

While the onion mixture is cooking, skin the chicken breasts, remove any connective tissue and cut the meat into chunks about 25mm square.

When the onion mixture is cooked, take the pan off the heat and remove the lid. Remove the chillies and cassia bark with a spoon and set aside. Now take a potato masher and thoroughly mash the onions, garlic and ginger until you get a fairly smooth purée.

Return the pan to the heat, still at its lowest setting, and add the ground coriander, ground cumin, chilli powder, turmeric and ground cloves.

Warm through the spices for about 1 minute, stirring all the time to mix them in thoroughly.

Raise the heat to medium and add the chicken chunks. Stir until they start to turn white at the edges. Return the chillies and cassia bark to the pan.

Add the red wine vinegar, tomato paste, black pepper, salt and 30ml water. Stir to mix all the ingredients and bring the mixture to a simmer.

Simmer the chicken for 15 minutes (less if you used small chunks).

If the mixture starts getting a little dry add 15ml water – no more just yet. As the chicken is cooking, add more water if the sauce gets too dry but, again, only 15ml at a time. If you like your curries very rich you could add 10ml ghee or vegetable oil to loosen the curry instead of 10ml water.

Check that the chicken is thoroughly cooked and remove the cassia bark. Leave the chillies in the curry as they make it look attractive when serving. You can always leave them on the side of the plate if you don't fancy eating them. Serve.

Tandoori-style Dishes

A tandoor is a large clay oven which is traditionally fired by wood or charcoal.

The tandoor is an ancient method of cooking bread and meat. Archaeologists have found examples of tandoors in the Indus Valley dating back to 1500 BC or even earlier. The tandoor originated in north and north-west India and Pakistan and was traditionally used for communal cooking. In more recent times the use of the tandoor has spread all over India and the rest of the world as a means of cooking in restaurants.

In their book, Classic Cooking of Punjab, Jiggs Kalra, Pushpesh Pant and Raminder Malhotra explain that tandoori cooking was spread by Punjabi refugees following the partition of India. Punjabis opened up roadside cafés or *dhaaba* and installed their tandoors to delight their customers. Large numbers of Punjabis emigrated and spread the use of the tandoor worldwide. In Britain, tandoori cooking became so popular that today almost all Indian restaurants offer tandoori dishes on their menus.

There can't be many people reading this book who have a tandoor in their kitchen so, sadly, we are not going to be able to make restaurant-style tandoori dishes. What we can do, though, is make a good approximation of tandoori cooking in a domestic oven and that's what the recipes achieve.

My tandoori chicken recipe uses chicken thighs rather than chicken quarters and the chicken tikka recipes use chicken mini-fillets rather than chunks of breast meat. The reason for both changes to the standard restaurant cuts is that they are more suited to cooking in a domestic oven and the chicken can cook right through without drying out. Not all the recipes in this chapter are cooked in the oven; Lamb Chops with Ginger are grilled and Karahi King Prawns are quickly fried in a hot karahi.

Chicken Tikka

Chicken Tikka is famous for being the key ingredients in Chicken Tikka Masala but these lovely tikkas are delicious on their own without a sauce. Served with naan bread and a salad they make a very pleasant lunch. Chicken Tikka also makes an easy supper dish accompanied by one of the vegetable bhajis.

You really do need to marinate the chicken mini-fillets for at least 2 hours but preferably for 4 hours. Marinating the chicken adds flavour and helps prevent the chicken from drying out in the oven. The marination does take the total preparation time to well over 1 hour, however, making the marinade doesn't take much time and once everything is in the fridge you can just go away and leave it. The cooking time itself is less than half an hour and once the chicken is in the oven it cooks away all by itself. You just need to turn over the mini-fillets a couple of times.

The use of red food colouring is entirely optional. It adds nothing to the taste of the tikkas but it does make them look just like the restaurant version and, to my eyes, very attractive. Simply leave out the colouring if you're not keen on using artificial ingredients and the chicken will come out the oven with a brownish colour rather than red. If you do decide to use red colouring then only powdered colouring will do. Liquid colouring (often used for cakes, etc.) will add too much liquid to get a deep enough colour and will make the marinade too watery.

ingredients

45ml Greek-style full fat yoghurt
30ml vegetable oil
1 small clove garlic – finely
    grated
finely grated ginger (about the
    same volume as the garlic)
5ml ground cumin seed

marination

Take a large bowl and add all the ingredients except the chicken mini-fillets.

Whisk the ingredients together until you get a smooth marinade.

If you are using the red food colouring powder add it now. Add the colouring only a tiny bit at a time, stir

¼ of a 2.5ml spoon *hot* chilli powder

2.5ml amchoor (dried mango powder)

1 pinch ground cloves

2 pinches ground cardamom seeds

3 grinds black peppercorns

2.5ml lemon juice

2.5ml sugar

salt

[optional] deep red food colouring powder

350g chicken mini-fillets

kitchen equipment

hand-held food grater with fine holes

large, shallow-sided baking tray

wire-mesh rack that fits inside the baking tray

tongs

well for the colouring to dissolve, check the colour and add a little more if necessary. The end result should be a lively deep pink, which will turn a warm red on cooking.

Cut out any white connective tissue and membrane from the chicken mini-fillets (kitchen scissors are ideal for this).

Add the mini-fillets to the marinade and stir thoroughly to get each one coated with marinade. Cover the bowl with cling film and marinate in the fridge for 2 - 4 hours.

cooking

Pre-heat your oven to Gas mark 7 / 220°C.

Take a large baking tray and line it with kitchen foil (optional but the foil saves you scraping burnt bits off the tray later). Sit a wire rack on the foil in the baking tray.

Use kitchen tongs to remove the chicken from the marinade and arrange the mini-fillets evenly over the wire rack.

Put the baking tray on a shelf in the upper part of the oven and bake the chicken for 8 minutes.

Remove the baking tray from the oven and, using tongs, turn over all the chicken mini-fillets. Return the tray to the oven and cook for another 8 minutes.

Now turn the mini-fillets back to the first side and cook for a final 6 minutes or until the chicken is completely cooked through and no pink meat remains. The chicken should have dark, almost burnt patches on the edges just like the version cooked in a tandoor.

Serve the chicken tikka on a bed of lettuce with naan bread, parathas or chapatis.

Tamarind Chicken Tikka

Tamarind Chicken Tikka are fully flavoured with a sweet and sour taste. They are absolutely delicious and come out a deep golden brown colour.

The chicken turns out much better if you marinate the mini-fillets for 4 hours but, if you're short of time, 2 hours will do. The marination adds flavour and helps prevent the chicken from drying out in the oven.

ingredients

30ml tamarind paste

30ml vegetable oil

1 small clove garlic – finely grated

2.5ml ground cumin seed

½ a 2.5ml spoon *hot* chilli powder

½ a 2.5ml spoon turmeric

2.5ml paprika

2 pinches ground cloves

⅓ of a 2.5ml spoon ground cardamom seeds (= the ground seeds of 2 green cardamom pods)

2 grinds black peppercorns

7.5ml sugar

salt (be careful how much you use – the tamarind paste will contain salt)

350g chicken mini-fillets

marination

Take a large bowl and add all the ingredients except the chicken mini-fillets.

If you don't have ready-ground cardamom seeds you will need to grind the seeds yourself. Split open 2 whole green cardamom pods and take out the little seeds. Now grind the seeds as best you can in a pestle and mortar. The result may be quite uneven but that's fine.

Whisk the ingredients together until you get a smooth marinade.

Cut out any white connective tissue from the chicken mini-fillets (kitchen scissors are ideal for this).

Add the mini-fillets to the marinade and stir thoroughly to get each one coated with the marinade. Marinate in the fridge for 2 - 4 hours.

cooking

Pre-heat your oven to Gas mark 7 / 220°C.

Take a large baking tray and line it with kitchen foil (optional but the foil saves you scraping burnt bits off the tray later). Sit a wire rack on the foil in the baking tray.

kitchen equipment

hand-held food grater with fine
  holes
pestle and mortar
large, shallow-sided baking tray
wire-mesh rack that fits inside
  the baking tray
tongs

Use kitchen tongs to remove the chicken from the marinade and arrange the mini-fillets evenly over the wire rack.

Put the baking tray on a shelf in the upper part of the oven and bake the chicken for 8 minutes.

Remove the baking tray from the oven and, using tongs, turn over all the chicken mini-fillets. Return the tray to the oven and cook for another 8 minutes.

Now turn the mini-fillets back over to the first side and cook for a final 6 minutes or until the chicken is completely cooked through and no pink meat remains. The chicken should have dark, almost burnt patches on the edges, just like the version cooked in a tandoor.

Serve the tamarind chicken tikka on a bed of lettuce with naan bread, parathas or chapatis.

Herb Chicken Tikka

These tikkas taste so fresh and they look very pretty too.

If you are having a party it's a great idea to make all 3 recipes for chicken tikka. The regular chicken tikkas are red, these are white speckled with green herbs and the tamarind tikkas are a golden brown. Together they look very attractive on a serving plate and provide a wonderful contrast of tastes.

The chicken comes out much better if you marinate the mini-fillets for 4 hours but, if you're short of time, 2 hours will do. The marination adds flavour and helps prevent the chicken from drying out in the oven.

ingredients

45ml Greek-style full fat yoghurt

30ml vegetable oil

1 small clove garlic – finely grated

finely grated ginger (about equal the volume of the garlic)

2.5ml ground coriander seed

⅓ of a 2.5ml spoon **hot** chilli powder

3 pinches ground cardamom seeds

3 grinds black peppercorns

5ml English mint sauce (preferably Colman's)

5ml lemon juice

5ml sugar

salt

15ml very finely chopped coriander leaves

350g chicken mini-fillets

marination

Take a large bowl and add all the ingredients except the chicken mini-fillets.

Whisk the ingredients together until you get a smooth, herby marinade.

Cut out any white connective tissue from the chicken mini-fillets (kitchen scissors are ideal for this).

Add the mini-fillets to the marinade and stir thoroughly to get each one coated with marinade. Cover the bowl with cling film and marinate in the fridge for 2 - 4 hours.

cooking

Pre-heat your oven to Gas mark 7 / 220°C.

Take a large baking tray and line it with kitchen foil (optional but the foil saves you scraping burnt bits off the tray later). Sit a wire rack on the foil in the baking tray.

Use kitchen tongs to remove the chicken from the marinade and arrange the mini-fillets evenly over the

kitchen equipment

hand-held food grater with fine
   holes
pestle and mortar
large, shallow-sided baking tray
wire-mesh rack that fits inside
   the baking tray
tongs

wire rack.

Put the baking tray on a shelf in the upper part of the oven and bake the chicken for 8 minutes.

Remove the baking tray from the oven and, using tongs, turn over all the chicken mini-fillets. Return the tray to the oven and cook for another 8 minutes.

Now turn the mini-fillets back over to the first side and cook for a final 6 minutes or until the chicken is completely cooked through and no pink meat remains. The chicken should have dark, almost burnt patches on the edges just like the version cooked in a tandoor.

Serve the herb chicken tikka on a bed of lettuce with naan bread, parathas or chapatis.

Tandoori-style Chicken

It is not possible to make authentic Tandoori Chicken in a domestic oven despite what some cookery books tell you. But you can make a respectable alternative and this recipe gives very good results.

The recipe is similar to the recipe for Chicken Tikka (just like in the restaurants) except that the marinade is smoother because the spices, including the garlic and ginger, are all dried and ground. The smooth marinade gives an authentic look to the cooked chicken. Restaurants usually use half a small chicken for their Tandoori Chicken but chicken thighs are more suitable for home cooking because we do not have the high heat of the tandoor to cook such a large joint of chicken quickly enough. So chicken thighs are ideal because they cook fairly quickly but still give the meat the essential "on the bone" flavour.

The use of red food colouring is entirely optional. It adds nothing to the taste of the dish but it does make it look just like the Tandoori Chicken you get in restaurants. Simply leave out the colouring if you're not keen on using artificial ingredients and the chicken will come out the oven with a brownish colour rather than red. If you do use red colouring you'll notice that once you get a deep pink colour in the marinade you would need to add lots more colouring to get a full red. You don't need the extra colouring as the marinade turns a deeper shade once it's cooked, so stop adding the red colouring the moment you first achieve that deep pink.

It is essential to marinate the chicken for at least 2 hours and preferably for 4 hours. A quick marination will not give the right results. You will see that there is oil in the marinade but please don't be tempted to reduce the amount shown in the recipe. The oil is essential as it bastes the chicken thighs while they are cooking. When the chicken thighs have finished cooking most of the oil will end up in the baking tray, not on your plate.

One way to help give you the smokiness of meat that has been cooked in a tandoor is to use smoked paprika instead of chilli powder. Smoked paprika will often be as hot as a mild chilli powder so you probably won't need to add much chilli powder to the marinade, if any.

And finally, please don't be put off by the long list of ingredients. There are no fresh ingredients to prepare and all the spices go into the marinade at the same time. You just have to make sure you've got everything in your kitchen cupboard before you start.

ingredients

45ml Greek-style full fat yoghurt

30ml vegetable oil

5ml water

2.5ml ground coriander seed

2.5ml ground cumin seed

2.5ml smoked paprika plus a little **hot** chilli powder if your smoked paprika is very mild

2.5ml amchoor (dried mango powder)

½ a 2.5ml spoon dried ginger powder

⅓ of a 2.5ml spoon dried garlic powder

1 pinch ground cinnamon

1 pinch ground cloves

1 pinch ground cardamom seeds

3 grinds black peppercorns

2.5ml red wine vinegar

2.5ml sugar

salt

[optional] deep red food colouring powder

4 large chicken thighs weighing about 475g in total

marination

Take a large bowl and add all the ingredients except the chicken thighs.

Whisk all the ingredients together until you get a smooth marinade.

If you are using the red food colouring add it now. Add the colouring only a tiny bit at a time, stir well, check the colour and add a little more if necessary. The end result should be a lively deep pink which will turn a deeper red on cooking.

Remove the skin from the chicken thighs by grabbing a loose end with some kitchen paper and pulling off the skin in one piece. Trim off any remaining bits of skin, fat and membrane from the chicken thighs.

Add the thighs to the marinade and stir thoroughly to get each one coated with the marinade. Cover with cling film and marinate in the fridge for 4 hours or for a minimum of 2 hours.

Remove the bowl from the fridge about half an hour before you want to start cooking.

cooking

Pre-heat your oven to Gas mark 7 / 220°C

Take a large baking tray and line it with kitchen foil (optional but the foil saves you scraping burnt bits off the tray later). Sit a wire rack on the foil in the baking tray.

Use kitchen tongs to remove the chicken from the

kitchen equipment

large, shallow-sided baking tray
wire-mesh rack that fits inside
    the baking tray
tongs

marinade, gently shake off any excess marinade and arrange the thighs on the wire rack with the bone side uppermost. Reserve the marinade.

Put the baking tray on a shelf in the upper part of the oven and bake the chicken for 15 minutes.

Remove the baking tray from the oven and, using tongs, turn over all the chicken thighs so that the smoother side is now facing upwards. Use a pastry brush to add a thin coat of marinade to the surface of the chicken thighs.

Return the tray to the oven and cook for a further 15 – 20 minutes or until the chicken is completely cooked through and the juices run clear (not pink) when the thighs are pierced with a skewer. The chicken should now have some dark, almost burnt, patches on the edges just as if it's been cooked in a tandoor.

Rest the chicken thighs for few minutes and then serve them on a bed of onion rings and green pepper rings with naan bread, paratha or chapatis.

Lamb Chops with Ginger

Lamb chops are not a common sight on the standard curry house menu, and more's the pity for that. You will need to go to a restaurant offering authentic South Asian cuisine to taste the delights of spicy lamb chops. You don't necessarily need to go upmarket though; your best bet is to try and find a simple Punjabi café.

When you come to eat the lamb chops you'll find the contrast between the soft meat, made extra tender by the marinade, and the crispy fat is just perfect.

If you can't get hold of English mint sauce, use very finely chopped fresh mint and add extra lemon juice and sugar.

An earlier version of this recipe first appeared on The Curry House website in a special feature on barbecuing South Asian style dishes. If you're making this dish in the summer, a barbecue grill is always a good alternative to the grill of a domestic cooker. The method is exactly the same except the heat is coming from the bottom not the top. In that case, brush a little of the marinade onto each side of the lamb chops as you turn them over on the barbecue.

ingredients

1 fat clove garlic - finely grated

5ml finely grated ginger

30ml vegetable oil

15ml lemon juice

5ml ground cumin seed

½ a 2.5ml spoon *hot* chilli
powder

2.5ml amchoor (dried mango
powder)

5ml English mint sauce
(preferably Colman's)

5ml sugar

3 grinds freshly ground black
peppercorns

marination

Take a bowl and add all the ingredients except the lamb chops.

Whisk the ingredients together until you get a smooth marinade.

Place the lamb chops in the rectangular dish and pour over the marinade. Scrape all the marinade out of the bowl with a rubber spatula.

Using one hand, roll the chops around in the marinade so each chop is completed coated. Arrange the chops in the dish in a single layer and cover the dish with cling film.

salt

4 lamb chops weighing 350g –
   375g in total

kitchen equipment

hand-held food grater with fine
   holes
rectangular dish which just
   holds the 4 lamb chops
rubber spatula

Marinate the lamb chops in the fridge for 4 hours or
for a minimum of 2 hours.

cooking

Pre-heat the grill in your cooker to medium-high.

Remove the lamb chops from the marinade and place
evenly over the rack of your grill pan. Reserve any
marinade left in the dish.

Grill the lamb chops on the first side for about 8
minutes (7 minutes for rarer chops and 9 minutes for
well done).

Turn over the lamb chops and brush with a little of
the reserved marinade.

Grill the second side of the chops for about another 8
minutes (7 minutes for rarer chops and 9 minutes for
well done).

Check that the lamb chops are how you like them -
medium-rare, medium or well done, and leave them to
rest for 2 minutes.

Serve on a bed of salad leaves.

Karahi King Prawns

I got the inspiration for this recipe from Sanjeev Kapoor's book Khana Khazana. Sanjeev is India's top TV chef and his books are always invaluable for new ideas because his recipes are authentically Indian rather than the westernised curry house adaptations we are used to.

Sanjeev's recipe was for Jhinga Varuval, which is crispy pan-fried prawns. I've altered the recipe to give it a taste reminiscent of the restaurant Patia.

It's important to use raw prawns which will be a grey colour and almost translucent. Ready-cooked prawns (which will be pink) will not work for this recipe as they will overcook and become tough and very chewy. If your prawns are frozen allow them to defrost slowly in the fridge until they are completely thawed before you cook them.

I tested a version of this dish where the prawns were marinated and then cooked under a grill but the method in this recipe gives far better results. The prawns take on an amazing sweet taste from being fried and then the sauce gives each prawn a sweet-and-sour coating. The trick to this recipe is to get everything prepared before you start cooking. Once you do start cooking the recipe is very quick and there's no time to do any more preparation.

ingredients

225g raw peeled jumbo king prawns – thawed if previously frozen

spring onions to garnish the prawns – use the long, thin kind

vegetable oil (see method for amounts)

1 small clove garlic – finely grated

Make sure the peeled jumbo king prawns are completely defrosted (if previously frozen). Dry the prawns thoroughly with kitchen paper. Cut out any black areas you find along the outside curved edge of the prawns.

Take the spring onions and cut off the root end, then cut them diagonally into slices about 2 - 3mm thick. Set aside to garnish the prawns.

Heat the karahi on a medium-high heat. Add sufficient oil so the karahi is coated with oil but there's no standing oil in the bottom of the pan. The oil should

finely grated ginger (about the
  same volume as the garlic)
2 "petals" from a star anise
5ml ground cumin seed
⅓ of a 2.5ml spoon *hot* chilli
  powder
5ml tomato paste
10ml tamarind paste
5ml lemon juice
5ml sugar
salt – be careful, the tamarind
  paste will contain salt and so
  may the prawns

kitchen equipment

hand-held food grater with fine
  holes
karahi or wok

be just starting to smoke a little.

Divide the prawns into 2 batches. Take the first batch of prawns and toss them into the hot karahi. Stir fry for 2 minutes or until the prawns have turned pink on the outside and white in the middle. By now there should be attractive little brown patches appearing on the sides of the prawns. Remove the prawns from the karahi and set aside on a large plate.

Add a few drops of oil to the karahi. When the oil is hot, stir fry the second batch of prawns in the same way as the first. When done, transfer the second batch of prawns to the plate. Set aside.

Remove the karahi from the heat and let it cool down a little. Turn the heat down to low.

Pour 10ml oil into the karahi and return it to the heat.

When the oil is hot slide the star anise, grated garlic and grated ginger into the karahi. Stir fry on low heat for about 1 minute and then pour 15ml water into the karahi.

Carefully tip the ground cumin seeds and chilli powder into the karahi. Try to make sure the spices land on the liquid and not the sides of the karahi or there is a risk that the spices will burn. Stir the ground spices into the liquid and warm them through for about 1 minute, stirring frequently.

Add the tomato paste, tamarind paste, lemon juice, sugar, salt (if using) and 45ml water to the karahi and stir to mix.

Simmer the mixture gently for about 10 minutes, by which time the sauce will have become thick and syrupy.

If the sauce starts to get too thick and there is a risk of it burning on the bottom of the karahi, add a little water. Do not add more than 5ml water at a time.

Taste the sauce and, if necessary, adjust the sweet/sour balance to your liking by adding more lemon juice or more sugar.

When the 10 minutes is up add the reserved prawns and cook, still on a low heat, for about 3 minutes or until the prawns are heated right through.

The sauce should now give a thick, glossy coating to the prawns. Remove the pieces of star anise and discard.

Serve on a bed of lettuce, garnished with the slices of spring onion.

Seekh Kebabs

Seekh kebabs are not, as some people think, named after the Sikh religion. The word *seekh* in this case means a skewer. Seekh kebabs are made from minced lamb mixed with herbs and spices and moulded into a sausage shape around a broad-bladed skewer.

I often make this Punjabi speciality for a quick supper served with parathas and a salad. You won't need skewers for this recipe because we are going to cook the kebabs in the oven. Once the kebabs are in the oven, you have nothing to do until they are ready. Don't overcook them or they will become very dry. This recipe makes six kebabs.

ingredients

350g minced lamb (20% fat content)

30ml Greek-style full fat yoghurt

1 clove garlic – finely grated

finely grated ginger (about double the volume of the garlic)

5ml ground coriander seed

5ml ground cumin seed

½ a 2.5ml spoon **hot** chilli powder

2.5ml paprika

3 pinches ground cardamom seeds

2 pinches ground cloves

2 grinds black peppercorns

5ml English mint sauce (preferably Colman's)

Put the minced lamb into a large bowl. Break up the lamb with a fork so there are no large lumps remaining.

Add all the other ingredients to the bowl and mix with the fork as best you can.

Now thoroughly mix all the ingredients together using your hands. Divide the mixture into 6 equal portions.

Take each portion of the mixture and roll it into a long thin sausage. The exact size doesn't matter but aim for kebabs which are about 25mm in diameter and 120mm long. Push in the ends to make them flat rather than pointed.

Pre-heat your oven to Gas mark 7 / 220°C.

Take a large baking tray and line it with kitchen foil (optional but the foil saves you scraping burnt bits off the tray later). Sit a wire rack on the foil in the baking tray.

15ml tomato paste

salt (about the same as you
would use in one of the
curries)

kitchen equipment

hand-held food grater with fine
holes

large, shallow-sided baking tray

wire-mesh rack that fits inside
the baking tray

Arrange the kebabs evenly over the wire rack.

Put the baking tray on a shelf in the upper part of the oven and bake the kebabs for about 24 minutes or until they are cooked right through, with no pink meat remaining.

Serve the kebabs on a bed of salad leaves with naan bread, parathas or chapatis.

Vegetable Bhajis

A bhaji or bhujia is a vegetable dish where the vegetables are cooked with spices but with very little sauce.

Mrs Balbir Singh, in her classic book Indian Cookery, explains the difference between vegetable curries and vegetable bhajis as follows: "Vegetable curries are prepared from single or a combination of two or more vegetables cooked in a gravy similar to that of meat curries. In the absence of the gravy the dish is known as a bhujia". Restaurants do not always follow this definition and you will find that many serve what are essentially vegetable curries with plenty of sauce but list them on the menu as vegetable bhajis.

There is another common problem of naming dishes. I know from letters I've received to my website, The Curry House, that people are often confused as to why onion bhajis, which are deep-fried onions mixed with batter, are called by the same name as other vegetable bhajis which come with a light sauce. It's a good question. Onion bhajis are really a type of pakora but Indian restaurants have used the term bhaji for them for so long now that the name has stuck.

I have included one recipe for a vegetable curry which you can easily adapt for other vegetables if you like. In my opinion, vegetable curries are fine if you are serving them with a tandoori dish or kebabs but I find that having a meat curry and a vegetable curry on the same plate gives you a kind of hybrid sauce which spoils the flavour of both.

In my experience too many restaurants let themselves down with their vegetable dishes. Their curries and tandoori dishes might be superb but their bhajis come to the table with overcooked vegetables swimming in oil. My vegetable bhaji recipes are made so the vegetables are cooked until just soft but enough to preserve their flavour and nutrients. The bhajis have a coating sauce and do not use excessive amounts of oil.

Oven-Baked Onion Bhajis

It's such a hassle to deep fry food at home and the results are at best variable and often quite poor because you can't keep the oil at a constant temperature. Then you have that "chip shop" smell of overheated fat in your house for days afterwards. So, what's the alternative if you want to make onion bhajis at home?

In my previous book I pan fried the bhajis and it produced pretty good results. But this time I've found an even better method, baking the bhajis in the oven. You do need to baste the bhajis with oil a couple of times while they are cooking but the total amount of oil in the finished bhaji is far less than for the deep-fried variety. The bhajis come out as flat discs rather than the ball-shaped ones you get in restaurants but they are no worse for that.

My onion bhajis are made with equal volumes of gram flour and self-raising wheat flour. Gram flour is made from Bengal gram which is also known as chana dhal and which is a relative of the chick pea. I have tested many versions of Oven-Baked Onion Bhajis and they do not taste right if you use wheat flour on its own. So if you can't get hold of gram flour I'm afraid you'll have to buy your onion bhajis from the supermarket.

Serve with any combination of Yoghurt Dip, Tamarind Dip, Onion Relish, Tomato Relish, mango chutney and lime pickle as a starter on their own or as an accompaniment to one of the curries.

ingredients

250g onions (trimmed weight) – sliced as in method
10ml vegetable oil

30ml gram flour
30ml self-raising flour
2.5ml ground coriander seed
2.5ml ground cumin seed

Trim and peel the onions and weigh out the required 250g. Cut the onions in half down from the tip to the root end. Place the onion halves cut-side down and slice quite thinly so you get lots of long thin strands of onion.

Heat the karahi on a high heat and add 10ml oil.

When the oil is hot add the onion slices and stir fry for about 3 minutes, breaking up the onion rings as you

⅓ of a 2.5ml spoon *hot* chilli
  powder
2.5ml turmeric
1 pinch ground cloves
2 pinches ground cardamom
  seeds
2 grinds black peppercorns
salt (use about the same as
  you'd use in one of the curries)

15ml finely chopped coriander
  leaves
45ml beaten egg

butter to oil the baking tray
vegetable oil to baste the bhajis
  before and during baking

kitchen equipment

karahi or wok
non-stick baking tray
pastry brush

stir.

Reduce the heat to low and continue stir frying the onions for another 7 minutes. By the end of the frying the onions should have taken on a golden colour without browning.

Turn off the heat and let the onions cool down a little.

Now take a mixing bowl, pour in all the dry ingredients and mix together.

Add the chopped coriander leaves, beaten egg and the fried onions from the karahi and stir thoroughly to bind the onion slices together with the stiff batter.

Pre-heat your oven to Gas Mark 6 / 200°C and let the onion batter rest for 10 minutes while the oven is heating up.

Take a non-stick baking tray and lightly butter the surface.

When the onion batter has rested for 10 minutes use something like a soup spoon to scoop out 4 portions of the onion batter. Place each portion on the baking tray leaving plenty of space between them. If some are larger than others just transfer some mixture between them until you get 4 roughly equal sized portions.

Shape each portion into a dome about 6cm across. It doesn't matter if you don't make perfect circles or if the edges are irregular. Now take a fork and poke around in the top of the bhajis so the surface is irregular and not flat (this increases the surface area and helps to make the top crunchy).

Pour some vegetable oil into a small bowl and, using a pastry brush, coat the top and the sides of each bhaji with oil.

Place the baking tray in the upper part of the hot oven and bake for 10 minutes.

Remove the baking tray from the oven and re-oil the bhajis with the pastry brush.

Bake for a further 10 minutes, remove the tray from the oven again and re-oil the bhajis one last time.

Put the baking tray back in the oven and bake for a final 10 minutes or until the bhajis are a deep brown colour and crunchy round the edges.

Serve immediately.

Bombay Aloo

You're unlikely to find a dish named Bombay Aloo outside of a restaurant menu or a supermarket shelf and even less likely to find a dish called Bombay Aloo in Mumbai (formerly Bombay) itself. But the name doesn't really matter. What you get served is hot, spicy potatoes flavoured with tomato and that style of dish can be found all over the Asian sub-continent.

It is important to choose the right potato when making this dish. Potatoes that are good for, say, making chips (fries) will be too fluffy and fall apart too easily. You need a variety that is good for boiling and which will stay firm after being cooked. I use a variety call Desirée.

Some restaurant versions of Bombay Aloo and most supermarket ones come with a tomato-rich sauce. My recipe is like the other bhajis in this chapter and has only a coating sauce.

ingredients

250g **boiling** potatoes (trimmed weight)

1 good-sized tomato

15ml vegetable oil
2 pinches mustard seeds
1 pinch cumin seeds
1 bay leaf
75g onions – finely chopped

1 small clove garlic
finely grated ginger (about the same volume as the grated garlic)

½ a 2.5ml spoon ground coriander seed

Bring a saucepan of water to the boil. Peel the potatoes and slice them into rounds about 18mm thick. Chop each round into rough cubes.

Slide the potato cubes into the boiling water, bring the water back to the boil and cook gently for 7 minutes.

Gently tip the potatoes into a sieve and, when the water has drained off, slide the potato cubes onto a large plate to dry off a little. Set aside.

Place the tomato in a bowl of boiling water and leave for 2 minutes. Remove the tomato and plunge it into cold water. Dry the tomato, slice it into quarters and peel off the skin. Remove the seeds and pith and then chop the tomato flesh into squares about 8mm across. Set aside.

Heat 15ml oil in the karahi on a medium-high heat. While the oil is heating up, finely chop the onion.

2.5ml ground cumin seed

⅓ of a 2.5ml spoon *hot* chilli powder

2.5ml turmeric

2.5ml lemon juice

2 grinds of black peppercorns

salt to taste (you'll need plenty)

water to loosen the sauce

10ml finely chopped coriander leaves

more finely chopped coriander leaves to garnish

kitchen equipment

hand-held food grater with fine holes

karahi or wok

saucepan to boil the potato cubes

When the oil is hot add the mustard seeds, cumin seeds and the bay leaf and stir to coat them with oil. Now add the chopped onions and stir fry for 5 minutes. The onions should end up brown around the edges but not burnt so lower the heat if necessary.

While the onions are frying, grate the garlic and ginger onto a small plate but make sure to give the onions a good stir from time to time so they don't start burning.

Now turn down the heat to low, let the pan cool down a little and then spoon the grated garlic and ginger into the pan. Stir in well and stir fry for 1 minute.

Pour 15ml water into the karahi and stir. Add the ground coriander, ground cumin, chilli powder and turmeric, making sure the ground spices hit the water and not the dry sides of the karahi where they might burn.

Warm through the spices for about 1 minute stirring all the time.

Add the lemon juice, black pepper, salt and 45ml water and stir to mix. Bring the water to simmering point and gently simmer the spicy liquid for about 5 minutes. Add 15ml more water if the karahi gets too dry but make sure the mixture is quite thick before you add the potatoes.

Slide the cubes of potato into the karahi and carefully stir them to coat them with the onions and spices. Use a metal spoon or a thin spatula to stir the bhaji as you do not want to break up the potato cubes.

Cook the bhaji, still on a low heat, for 5 minutes, stirring gently from time to time so the potato cubes cook right through.

Add the chopped tomatoes and 10ml chopped coriander leaves. Stir to mix and cook for 2 minutes.

Stir the bhaji a couple of times in the final 2 minutes to heat through the tomato pieces.

Remove the bay leaf and discard.

Serve garnished with more finely chopped coriander leaves.

Cauliflower Bhaji

According to food historian Dr. K.T. Achaya "phool-gobhi" or cauliflower was introduced to India by the British in the mid 19th century. Although the British intended it for their own use it has since become widely cultivated and is now used in everyday cooking.

All restaurants have a cauliflower bhaji on their menu and it is a very popular vegetable side dish. Unlike the restaurant version, my recipe has very little sauce because it is a true bhaji, not a cauliflower curry. It is lightly spiced but the recipe really brings out the sweet flavour of the cauliflower.

ingredients

250g cauliflower (trimmed weight)

20ml vegetable oil

75g onion – finely chopped

½ a 2.5ml spoon finely grated ginger

½ a 2.5ml spoon ground coriander seed

½ a 2.5ml spoon ground cumin seed

3 pinches **hot** chilli powder

½ a 2.5ml spoon turmeric

2 grinds of black peppercorns

salt to taste

water to loosen the sauce

Wash the cauliflower and cut it into large florets 25 - 35mm across at the widest part.

Bring a saucepan of water to the boil and add the cauliflower florets. Bring the water back to the boil and cook for 10 minutes.

Gently tip the cauliflower florets into a sieve and, when the water has drained, slide the florets onto a large plate to dry off a little. Set aside.

While the cauliflower is cooking, finely chop the onion. Finely grate the ginger onto a small plate.

Heat 20ml oil in a karahi on a medium heat. When the oil is hot add the chopped onion and stir fry for 5 minutes until the pieces of onion are translucent but not brown. Lower the heat if the onions start to fry too hard.

Turn the heat to low and add the grated ginger. Stir fry for 1 minute.

Pour 15ml water into the karahi, stir and then add the ground coriander, ground cumin, chilli powder and turmeric. Make sure the ground spices hit the water

kitchen equipment

hand-held food grater with fine
   holes
karahi or wok
large saucepan to cook the
   cauliflower

and not the dry sides of the karahi where they might burn.

Warm through the spices for about 1 minute stirring all the time.

Add the black pepper, salt and 45ml more water. Bring the water to simmering point and gently simmer the spicy liquid for about 10 minutes. Add 15ml more water if the karahi gets too dry but make sure the mixture is quite thick before you add the cauliflower.

Add the cooked cauliflower florets to the karahi and carefully stir them to coat them with the oil and spices. Use a metal spoon or a thin spatula to stir the bhaji as you do not want to break up the cauliflower.

Cook on a low heat for 5 minutes. Stir carefully a couple of times to make sure the cauliflower is heated right through. Serve.

Bhindi Bhaji

Okra is an odd vegetable. It is a member of the mallow family but, if you cut one open, it looks a bit like a chilli with all the little white seeds inside. Inside too is a thick gum which doesn't look at all appetising to eat, nor will it be unless you cook the okra properly. Frying the okra first, as long as it is completely dry after washing, helps to neutralise the sticky gum and you can then afford to add some liquid in the second stage of the cooking without the whole sauce looking like glue.

Okra has many names, including *bhindi* in Hindi and Urdu, *gumbo* in Creole and *ladies' fingers* for the old British colonials in India. Yet it originates from neither India, nor the Americas or Britain but is a native of Africa.

Bhindi Bhaji has been on the Indian restaurant menu for as long as I can remember. When I first tried it in the 1970s it seemed very exotic and quite unlike any of the common British vegetables. I still enjoy it but too many restaurants cook okra to a soft mush and smother it in too much oily sauce. In this recipe the okra still has some texture and the tomato coating brings a fresh taste to the bhaji.

ingredients

200g okra (untrimmed weight)
1 good-sized tomato
15ml vegetable oil to fry the okra

1 small clove garlic – finely grated
finely grated ginger (about the same volume as the garlic)
10ml vegetable oil to fry the garlic and ginger

Wash the okra, drain off any excess water and dry thoroughly with kitchen paper.

Cut off the stalk area well into the fleshy part and slice off the pointed end.

Slice the okra crossways into sections about 20mm wide and set aside.

Place the tomato in a bowl of boiling water and leave for 2 minutes. Remove the tomato and plunge it into cold water. Dry the tomato, slice it into quarters and peel off the skin. Remove the seeds and pith and then chop the tomato flesh into squares about 8mm across. Set aside.

2.5ml ground coriander seed

½ a 2.5ml spoon ground cumin seed

¼ of a 2.5ml spoon **hot** chilli powder

½ a 2.5ml spoon turmeric

2 pinches ground cardamom seeds

2 grinds of black peppercorns

salt to taste

water to loosen the sauce

kitchen equipment

hand-held food grater with fine holes

karahi or wok

Finely grate the garlic and ginger onto a small plate.

Heat 15mm oil in the karahi on a medium-high heat.

When the oil is hot, slide the pieces of okra into the karahi and stir fry for 5 minutes.

Remove the fried okra from the karahi and set aside on a clean plate.

Let the karahi cool down a bit, return it to a low heat and add 10ml oil. Add the grated ginger and garlic and stir fry for 1 minute.

Pour 15ml water into the karahi, stir and then add the ground coriander, ground cumin, chilli powder, turmeric and ground cardamom seeds. Make sure the ground spices hit the water and not the dry sides of the karahi where they might burn.

Warm through the spices for about 1 minute, stirring all the time.

Add the black pepper, salt and 45ml water. Bring the water to simmering point and gently simmer the spicy liquid for about 5 minutes. Add 15ml more water if the karahi gets too dry but make sure the mixture is quite thick before you add the chopped tomatoes.

Add the chopped tomatoes to the karahi, bring back to a simmer and then add the reserved pieces of okra.

Gently heat the okra and tomatoes for a final 5 minutes. The okra should still have a little bite to it but if you like your okra very soft you will need to continue the cooking for a short while. If so, you may need to add a little more water to finish the cooking. Serve.

Tarka Dhal

This recipe for Tarka Dhal is from my first book: The Curry House Cookery Book. I tried dozens of different ways to make tarka dhal when writing that book and this was the best one by far. I have made some changes to the spicing and the method to reflect the way I make it now and I think the revisions make the dhal even better.

Tarka is a flavouring of garlic or onions which are cooked in oil with spices and used to garnish plain boiled dhal. Dhal is the general name for any of the dried pulses – lentils, peas and beans. The hot tarka is poured over the cooked lentils just before serving.

Restaurants tend to make their tarka dhal like a curry and so cook everything together. That's the way my recipe does it too.

This recipe works well as the basis for an egg and lentil curry. Make the tarka dhal as described in the method and serve topped with 3 hard boiled eggs (still warm) with each egg cut in half. To make it even more interesting, you could add some chopped fresh tomato pieces (where the tomatoes have been skinned and de-seeded) and some finely chopped coriander leaves to the dhal 5 minutes before the end of the cooking.

If you fancy using crispy onion slices as a garnish then there is really no need to make your own. It's far easier and just as good to buy a pack of crispy onions which you can often find in supermarkets along with the soups.

ingredients

100g split red lentils (masoor dhal)
500ml water to cook the lentils
30ml butter

5ml vegetable oil
2 cloves garlic – sliced as in method

Weigh 100g red lentils and pour them into a measuring jug. Place the jug under running cold water and wash the lentils. Once the jug is full let the lentils settle and then pour out most of the water without losing any lentils. Repeat the washing process 4 or 5 times. Finally, drain the lentils into a sieve.

Tip the washed lentils into a large saucepan containing 500ml cold water and bring the water to the boil. Once the water is boiling, carefully skim off

2.5ml ground coriander seed

5ml ground cumin seed

⅔ of a 2.5ml spoon *hot* chilli
  powder

2.5ml turmeric

2 grinds black peppercorns

salt to taste (you will need plenty
  as lentils are very bland)

water to loosen the sauce

[optional] 15ml butter to loosen
  the dhal

[optional] crispy onion slices to
  garnish

finely chopped coriander leaves
  to garnish

kitchen equipment

18cm saucepan to boil the
  lentils

20cm heavy-bottomed pan

any froth that gathers on top the water. Add 30ml butter to the water and stir to melt.

Cook the lentils with a vigorous boil for 10 minutes and then turn the heat down to a simmer. Do not cover the pan.

While the dhal is cooking, trim and peel the cloves of garlic. Cut the garlic crossways into thin slices and then cut each slice into thin strips.

Simmer the lentils until most of the water has evaporated or has been absorbed by the lentils (about a further 12 minutes). Stir the lentils regularly in the final stages of the cooking so they don't burn on the bottom of the pan as the water is used up.

Remove the pan of dhal from the heat and cover with a lid until needed.

Heat 5ml oil in a 20cm heavy-bottomed saucepan over a medium/low heat.

Slide the garlic slices into the pan and fry, stirring continuously, until the garlic is just turning brown and is giving off a smoky aroma. Now quickly add 60ml of the cooked dhal to the pan to stop the garlic burning.

Reduce the heat to low and let the pan cool down, by which time all the sizzling will have stopped. Then add the ground coriander, ground cumin, chilli powder and turmeric. Stir to mix and warm through the spices for about 30 seconds.

Add the remaining dhal and any liquid left in the pan. Add the black pepper and salt and stir to mix all the ingredients together.

Bring the dhal to the boil and simmer gently for 15 minutes, stirring from time to time. Taste the dhal and add more salt if necessary.

If the dhal gets too thick add 15ml water - no more just yet. As the dhal is cooking add more water if necessary but only 15ml at a time. The final texture should be thick but still fluid. If you like your dhal very rich (I do) you can add 15ml butter instead of 15ml water. The tarka dhal in most restaurants will contain considerably more fat even if you add this extra amount.

Transfer the dhal to a warmed serving dish and garnish with some finely chopped coriander leaves and some crispy onion slices (if using).

Brinjal Bhaji

The *brinjal* or aubergine is a large fruit with a glossy purple skin. At least some aubergines are that size and colour; an alternative name of "eggplant" gives us a hint that some of the aubergine family are smaller and have white skins. In Thai cooking, tiny aubergines the size and colour of green peas are also used.

In too many restaurants Brinjal Bhaji has the dubious honour of being the oiliest dish on the menu. The flesh of the aubergine acts like a sponge and soaks up almost as much oil as you can throw at it. So, if the aubergine is carelessly cooked, it will hold all that oil and then give it up later in the serving dish when things starts to cool down.

Fried aubergine is delicious but to avoid having to use too much oil I have suggested cooking the aubergine in two stages. First the aubergine pieces are stir fried in some hot oil to bring out the flavour. Then they are simmered with fried onions and spices until tender. Make sure the pieces of aubergine are soft before you serve them. If undercooked, aubergines have an unpleasant texture when you bite into them.

ingredients

20ml vegetable oil to fry the
    aubergine
1 purple aubergine (about 275g
    untrimmed weight)
1 good-sized tomato

15ml vegetable oil to fry the
    onion and whole spices
2 pinches kalonji
1 pinch fennel seeds
75g onions – finely chopped
1 small clove garlic

Wash and dry the aubergine and cut it crossways into slices about 20mm thick, discarding the top and tail pieces. Take each slice and cut it in half and then cut each half into wedges about 20mm across at the widest point.

Put the tomato into a bowl of boiling water and leave for 2 minutes. Remove the tomato and plunge it into cold water. Dry the tomato, slice it into quarters and peel off the skin. Remove the seeds and pith and then chop the tomato flesh into squares about 8mm across. Set aside.

Heat 20ml oil in a karahi on a medium-high heat.

finely grated ginger (about the same volume as the grated garlic)

½ a 2.5ml spoon ground coriander seed

2.5ml ground cumin seed

¼ of a 2.5ml spoon **hot** chilli powder

½ a 2.5ml spoon turmeric

2 grinds of black peppercorns

salt to taste

water to cook the aubergines and loosen the sauce

10ml finely chopped coriander leaves

more finely chopped coriander leaves to garnish

kitchen equipment

hand-held food grater with fine holes

karahi or wok

When the oil is hot, slide the aubergine wedges into the karahi and stir fry for 7 minutes until the flesh is covered in brown speckles.

While the aubergine wedges are frying finely chop the onion.

Remove the aubergine wedges from the karahi at the end of the 7 minutes, transfer to a bowl and cover.

Keep the heat at medium-high and pour 15ml oil into the karahi.

When the oil is hot, add the kalonji and fennel seeds and stir to coat them in oil. Now add the chopped onions and stir fry for 5 minutes. The onions should end up brown around the edges but not burnt.

While the onions are frying, grate the garlic and ginger onto a small plate but make sure to give the onions a good stir from time to time so they don't start burning.

Now turn down the heat to low, let the pan cool down a little and then spoon the grated garlic and ginger into the pan. Stir in well and stir fry for 1 minute.

Pour 15ml water into the karahi and stir. Add the ground coriander, ground cumin, chilli powder and turmeric, making sure the ground spices hit the water and not the dry sides of the karahi where they might burn.

Warm through the spices for about 1 minute, stirring all the time.

Add the black pepper and salt and stir to mix.

Slide the reserved aubergine wedges into the karahi and pour in 60ml water. Stir to mix thoroughly.

Raise the heat to bring the water to the boil and then turn the heat down again so the liquid is just simmering.

Cook the aubergine wedges for 10 minutes, stirring carefully from time to time. Use a metal spoon or a thin spatula to stir the bhaji because you do not want to mash up the aubergine wedges once they start getting soft. Add 15ml more water if the karahi gets too dry but make sure the mixture is quite thick before you add the tomato chunks.

Check whether the aubergine pieces are soft. If not, you may need to add a little water and simmer for a few more minutes.

When the aubergine wedges are soft, add the chopped tomatoes and 10ml chopped coriander leaves. Stir to mix, raise the heat until everything starts to sizzle a bit and then reduce the heat back to low and cook for 2 minutes.

Stir the bhaji very gently a couple of times in the final 2 minutes so the tomato pieces are heated right through.

Serve garnished with more finely chopped coriander leaves.

Mushroom Bhaji

I am not a great fan of the mushroom bhajis that are served in Indian restaurants. The sliced mushrooms they use often end up chewy because they have been overcooked and the sauce overwhelms the taste of the mushrooms.

Mushrooms are one of those vegetables, like cabbage, that should be cooked either very quickly or very slowly. Large mushrooms which have been sliced are excellent when added to a stew where the long, slow cooking allows the mushrooms to season the sauce. But, for a quickly cooked bhaji, I think you need to use whole button mushrooms which will come out soft and full of taste.

This recipe is very quick and should only be made at the last minute, otherwise the mushrooms will overcook and their texture will be ruined.

ingredients

5ml vegetable oil to fry the
  mushrooms
175g button mushrooms

10ml vegetable oil to fry the
  onions
50g red onion – finely chopped
1 small clove garlic – finely
  grated
finely grated ginger (about the
  same volume as the garlic)

½ a 2.5ml spoon ground
  coriander seed
½ a 2.5ml spoon ground cumin
  seed
3 pinches *hot* chilli powder
¼ of a 2.5ml spoon turmeric
1 pinch ground cardamom seeds

Wipe the mushrooms clean with some damp kitchen paper. Leave the mushrooms whole and do not peel off the outer layer. Dry the mushrooms thoroughly with dry kitchen paper.

Trim and finely chop the red onion. If you don't have a red onion, use a regular onion.

Heat 5ml oil in a karahi on a high heat.

When the oil is hot, slide the mushrooms into the karahi and stir fry for 5 minutes until the mushrooms have attractive brown patches on their white surfaces.

Remove the mushrooms from the karahi and set aside on a plate. Reduce the heat to medium.

Return the karahi to the heat and add 10ml oil.

When the oil is hot add the chopped onions and stir fry for 5 minutes. The onions should end up brown around the edges but not burnt.

While the onions are frying, grate the garlic and ginger onto a small plate but make sure to give the

2 grinds of black peppercorns

2.5ml lemon juice

water to loosen the sauce

10ml finely chopped coriander
  leaves

more finely chopped coriander
  leaves to garnish

kitchen equipment

hand-held food grater with fine
  holes

karahi or wok

onions a good stir from time to time so they don't start burning.

Now turn the heat to low, let the pan cool a little and then spoon the grated garlic and ginger into the pan. Stir in well and stir fry for 1 minute.

Pour 20ml water into the karahi and stir. Add the ground coriander, ground cumin, chilli powder, turmeric and ground cardamom seeds, making sure the ground spices hit the water and not the dry sides of the karahi where they might burn.

Warm through the spices for about 1 minute, stirring all the time to mix them in thoroughly.

Add the black pepper, salt, lemon juice and 60ml water. Bring the water to simmering point and gently simmer the onions and spices for about 7 minutes. Add 15ml more water if the karahi gets too dry but make sure the mixture is quite thick before you add the mushrooms.

Add 10ml finely chopped coriander leaves and stir to mix. Now add the reserved mushrooms (and any liquid that has collected on the plate), stir and cook for about 3 minutes until the mushrooms are hot and any liquid has evaporated.

Serve immediately, garnished with a sprinkling of finely chopped coriander leaves.

Saag Bhaji

Saag Bhaji cooks very quickly, so make sure you have everything prepared and measured out before you start. The bhaji is quite garlicky but not very spicy as you don't want to overpower the fresh taste of the spinach.

Make sure you grate fresh nutmeg for this bhaji. I did a test using ground mace but it needs a longer cooking time in plenty of sauce. In a stir-fry like this, ground mace comes out with an unpleasantly gritty texture.

Sometimes this dish is called Palak Bhaji in restaurants. Saag can refer to a variety of green leaves, including fresh fenugreek leaves, whereas palak refers specifically to spinach. My recipe is different from the Saag Bhaji you'll find in many Indian restaurants which are really spinach curries where the spinach has been seriously overcooked. Here, fresh spinach is stir fried in butter until it is just tender.

ingredients

200g fresh baby leaf spinach
  (ready washed)

5ml vegetable oil
1 clove garlic – sliced as in
  method

½ a 2.5ml ground cumin seed
3 pinches *hot* chilli powder
2 passes of a whole nutmeg on a
  very fine nutmeg grater

2 grinds of black peppercorns
salt to taste
2.5ml lemon juice

water to loosen the sauce

Spread out the spinach leaves on plenty of kitchen paper. Place more kitchen paper on top of the spinach and gently pat down until the spinach leaves are as dry as possible. If your spinach wasn't pre-washed then wash the leaves in a bowl of cold water, transfer the leaves to a colander to drain off any excess water and then proceed as before.

When the spinach leaves are as dry as possible transfer them to a bowl so you can quickly empty them into the karahi when the time comes.

Trim and peel the clove of garlic. Cut the garlic into thin slices and then cut each slice into thin strips.

Heat 5ml vegetable oil in the karahi over a medium heat.

Slide the garlic slices into the pan and fry, stirring continuously, until the garlic starts to turn brown at the edges. Now quickly add 20ml water to stop the

15ml butter (at room
temperature)

kitchen equipment

karahi or wok

garlic burning.

Turn the heat to low and add the ground cumin, chilli
powder and ground nutmeg. Stir to mix and warm
through the spices for about 30 seconds.

Add the black pepper, salt, lemon juice and 45ml
water. Bring the water to simmering point and gently
simmer the spicy liquid for about 7 minutes. Add
15ml more water if the karahi gets too dry but make
sure the sauce is as thick as possible before you add
the spinach.

Now you need to work quickly.

Turn the heat to high, add 15ml butter and stir
vigorously to melt the butter.

When the butter has melted add the spinach leaves
and stir fry until the leaves have wilted but the stalks
are still just a little crunchy.

Transfer the spinach to a warmed serving dish and
serve immediately.

You may find that the spinach drops some liquid in
the serving dish. If you like, you can transfer the
spinach to your plate with a slotted spoon so the
liquid is left in the serving dish. But I find the garlicky,
buttery liquid is very nice mopped up with some naan
bread or chapati.

Aloo Gobi

Aloo Gobi is a vegetable curry made with potatoes and cauliflower. The other vegetable recipes in this chapter are bhajis with only a coating sauce but this recipe is made as a curry so has a full quantity of sauce.

Parboiling the potatoes and cauliflower speeds up the cooking time and helps to keep the vegetables from breaking up after you add them to the sauce. Make sure you use a good boiling potato that will stay firm when boiled and have a waxy texture (I use a variety called Desirée) and not one that is best for roast potatoes or chips (fries).

I think Aloo Gobi goes really well with any of the tandoori-style dishes and also with Garlic Chicken and King Prawn Sizzler in the chapter on House Specials, because all those dishes are relatively dry. I prefer the drier vegetable bhajis as accompaniments to the Curry House Favourites and the other House Specials. But that's just my personal preference because I'm not keen on different sauces mingling together on my plate.

ingredients

45ml vegetable oil
250g onions – finely chopped
2 cloves garlic – finely grated
grated ginger (about half the
   volume of the garlic)
60ml water

200g **boiling** potatoes (trimmed
   weight)
200g cauliflower (trimmed
   weight)

5ml ground coriander seed
7.5ml ground cumin seed
½ a 2.5ml spoon **hot** chilli

Heat 45ml oil in the heavy-bottomed pan on a medium heat. While the oil is heating up, finely chop 250g onion.

When the oil is hot, add the chopped onion to the pan and stir fry for 5 minutes. The onions should not brown, so lower the heat a little if they start to fry too hard.

While the onions are frying, grate the garlic and ginger onto a small plate but make sure to give the onions a good stir from time to time so they don't start browning.

Spoon the grated garlic and ginger into the pan (plus any juices left on the plate). Stir in well and stir fry continuously for 2 minutes.

Add 60ml water and mix in thoroughly.

powder

2.5ml turmeric

2 pinches ground cloves

2 pinches ground cardamom
   seeds

2.5ml lemon juice

5ml tomato paste

2 grinds of black peppercorns

salt to taste

water to loosen the sauce

2 pinches dried fenugreek
   (*kazuri methi*) leaves

[optional] 15ml ghee or
   vegetable oil

kitchen equipment

hand-held food grater with fine
   holes

potato masher

20cm heavy-bottomed pan

Once the liquid starts to boil put a lid on the pan, turn the heat down to minimum and cook for 20 minutes. Do not remove the lid during this time.

While the onion mixture is cooking, take a large saucepan, fill it ¾ full of water and get the water boiling.

Wash and peel the potatoes and weigh out the required 200g. Slice the potatoes into rounds about 18mm thick. Chop each round into rough cubes.

Wash the cauliflower and weigh out the required 200g. Cut the cauliflower into florets about 25mm across at the widest part.

When the water comes to a boil, carefully lower the potato cubes and cauliflower florets into the water. Return the water to the boil and simmer the vegetables for 10 minutes. Drain the vegetables into a sieve and then gently tip them onto a large plate to dry off a little.

When the onion mixture is cooked, take the pan off the heat and remove the lid. Now take a potato masher and thoroughly mash the onions, garlic and ginger until you get a fairly smooth purée.

Return the pan to the heat, still at its lowest setting, and add the ground coriander, ground cumin, chilli powder, turmeric, ground cloves and ground cardamom seeds.

Warm through the spices for about 1 minute, stirring all the time to mix them in thoroughly.

Add the lemon juice, tomato paste, black pepper, salt and 30ml water. Stir to mix all the ingredients and bring the mixture to a simmer.

Simmer the sauce for 10 minutes.

If the mixture starts getting a little dry, add 15ml

water – no more just yet. As the sauce cooks add more water if it gets too dry but, again, only 15ml at a time.

When the 10 minutes is up, add the dried fenugreek leaves to the sauce and stir to mix.

Now add the cooked vegetables to the sauce and stir in very gently with a metal tablespoon. Don't use a thick wooden or plastic spoon or you risk breaking up the vegetables as you stir them.

Make sure the vegetables are completely coated in sauce and bring the sauce back to a gentle simmer. Simmer for 5 minutes. Gently stir the vegetables a couple of times as they finish cooking.

If the sauce starts to get too thick, add another 15ml water and gently stir it into the curry. If you like your curries very rich you could add 15ml ghee or vegetable oil to loosen the sauce instead of 15ml water. Serve.

Rice and Bread

I have deliberately limited the number of recipes for rice dishes and breads to those which are most popular and easiest to make.

For example, I have not included a recipe for biryani. There are recipes for a selection of biryanis in my previous book, The Curry House Cookery Book, but although they are delicious to eat they take far longer than an hour to make and so are not suitable for this book. Nor have I included recipes for the more elaborate breads such as Peshawari Naan or Stuffed Paratha. Again, you will find the recipes in my previous book.

For this book, there are two exceptions to the rule that the recipes have to be made from start to finish in under an hour. They are the bread recipes and the tandoori-style dishes. With the bread recipes, the dough has to be left to either rise or rest before it can be used. While the dough is rising or resting you have nothing else to do, so the recipe needs far less than an hour of your attention. The same goes for the tandoori-style dishes which need a few hours to marinate.

You will notice that the full title of the naan recipe is *griddled* Naan. There aren't many of us who have a tandoor in their kitchen and cooking naan in a domestic oven just doesn't work. I have tested scores of naan bread recipes and none of the ones cooked in an oven came out with a crispy base and a soft top like an authentic tandoori naan. However, by using a cast-iron griddle and my recipe you can get results that are very close to the real thing.

My recipe for Pilau Rice gives you the option of using food colouring powder to create the look of the pilau rice served in many restaurants with its kaleidoscope of white, red and yellow grains. You can leave out the colouring if you wish because it does nothing for the flavour of the rice. The flavour comes from the fragrant Basmati rice itself and from the whole spices used in the cooking.

Pilau Rice

This is a much quicker version of Pilau Rice than the one which appeared in The Curry House Cookery Book and can easily be made in under an hour.

When you are boiling the rice you should have as little contact with it as possible so that you don't burst the grains and release the starch. You don't have to be quite so careful when you stir fry the rice with the spices in the second phase of the cooking as the rice grains will have firmed up while they were resting.

Using food colouring is entirely optional. It does make the rice look attractive and I do use it at home but it does nothing for the taste of the pilau rice, so you can very easily leave it out if you wish. You cannot use liquid food colouring for pilau rice as it adds too much liquid and spreads the colour too widely. If you can't get hold of powdered food colouring you will have to omit it anyway.

You can remove the whole spices from the rice just before you serve if you wish. Personally, I like the look of the spices in the rice and most people these days understand that you just push them to the side of the plate while eating.

Try and use the best quality Basmati rice you can afford. It will repay you with its wonderful flavour.

ingredients

125g best quality Basmati rice – **do not** wash or soak the rice

10ml vegetable oil or ghee
35mm piece of cassia bark
3 whole green cardamom pods
3 whole cloves
salt

[optional] yellow food colouring powder

Take the largest saucepan you own and fill it with cold water, leaving about 5cm between the water level and the top of the pan. Do not add salt at this stage. Put a lid on the pan and bring the water to the boil.

Remove the lid from the pan and sprinkle the rice slowly into the boiling water. Make sure you don't dump the rice in the water in one go or you will end up with lumps of rice.

Gently stir the rice once to distribute the grains evenly over the base of the pan and adjust the heat so the water is only **just** simmering. **Do not** let the water

[optional] red food colouring
  powder

kitchen equipment

large saucepan to boil the rice
karahi or wok to fry the rice

boil vigorously.

Cook the rice for about 12 minutes. Do not stir the rice again. Test the rice regularly after about 11 minutes and remove the pan from the heat at the point where the rice is going from a little hard to just soft in the middle.

Pour the rice into a sieve and drain off the water.

When no more water is draining off, gently tip the rice onto a large plate. Use a fork to carefully spread the rice evenly across the plate. Set it aside to allow the rice to firm up a little – this takes about 10 minutes.

While the rice is firming up, take a karahi and pour in 10ml vegetable oil or ghee, the cassia bark, cardamom pods and whole cloves. Place the karahi over a low heat and gently warm through the spices, stirring from time to time.

When the spices are giving off a warm, aromatic fragrance and the rice has finished resting, slide the cooked rice into the karahi.

Sprinkle the salt over the rice and carefully stir it so the grains are lightly coated in oil.

If you are using the food colouring powder now is the time to add it. Otherwise, omit the next two steps.

Take a teaspoon and pick up a tiny amount of yellow food colouring powder on the very tip of the spoon. Do not sprinkle it over the rice but dump it all in one place. Do the same with some red food colouring powder on a different area of rice. Leave the colouring to soak in for about 30 seconds without stirring the rice at all.

Now stir the rice to distribute the food colouring. You should find that some grains are strongly coloured, others are a lightly coloured and most are still white. If you haven't added enough colouring add a tiny bit more and repeat the procedure.

Spread out the rice over the surface of the karahi so it dries out and begins to gently fry. Heat the rice in the karahi, still on a low heat, for about 8 minutes stirring from time to time and then spreading out the rice once again.

Serve the rice in a warmed serving dish. You can leave in the whole spices or remove them – it's up to you.

If you want to keep the rice on hold while your curry finishes cooking, tightly cover the serving dish and place it in the oven at 170°C/Gas Mark 3 for up to 20 minutes.

Plain Rice

Here are step by step instructions for how to cook perfect plain Basmati rice.

ingredients

125g best quality Basmati rice –
  do not wash or soak the rice
salt

kitchen equipment

large saucepan to boil the rice

Take the largest saucepan you own and fill it with cold water, leaving about 5cm between the water level and the top of the pan. Do not add salt at this stage. Put a lid on the pan and bring the water to the boil.

Remove the lid from the pan and sprinkle the rice slowly into the boiling water. Make sure you don't dump the rice in the water in one go or you will end up with lumps of rice.

Gently stir the rice once to distribute the grains evenly over the base of the pan and adjust the heat so the water is only **just** simmering. **Do not** let the water boil vigorously.

Cook the rice for about 12 minutes. Do not stir the rice again. Add some salt to the water after about 10 minutes cooking.

Test the rice regularly after about 11 minutes and remove the pan from the heat at the point where the rice is going from a little hard to just soft in the middle.

Pour the rice into a sieve and drain off the water.

Serve the rice in a warmed serving dish.

If you want to keep the rice on hold while your curry finishes cooking, tightly cover the serving dish and place it in the oven at 170°C/Gas Mark 3 for up to 20 minutes.

griddled Naan

The first thing to say about making naan bread at home is that you will never be able to make soft, fluffy naan bread like the ones that come out of a tandoor oven. You cannot get that sort of heat in a domestic oven and you won't get the naan infused with all the smoky meat juices that drip down onto the charcoal.

But... you can make a very respectable alternative using a cast-iron griddle. Because you are using a griddle the naan is made in a circle so it fits the griddle perfectly rather than in the traditional tear-drop shape.

There has been plenty of discussion and quite a bit of experimentation from subscribers to The Curry House Premium Area on the subject of my naan recipe from The Curry House Cookery Book (which I have completely revised for this book). There were two main topics of discussion:

- can naan bread successfully be made in a domestic oven?
- the dried yeast used in the recipe may give a yeasty taste to the bread – can this be eliminated?

I have firmly established that the answer to the first question is "no". When I was creating the recipe for my first book I conducted many, many experiments while researching the naan bread recipe and did not once come near to a decent result when using a domestic oven. All of them ended up with a noticeable bread-like crust and not one with the characteristic soft top/crispy base of a tandoor-cooked naan.

The answer to the second issue is yes, the yeasty taste can be reduced or even eliminated but at some cost to convenience. For the recipe below I have reduced the quantity of dried yeast to the absolute minimum that is guaranteed to work and I am very pleased with the result. But all bread made with dried yeast will have a faint yeasty flavour and the only way to eliminate that is to use fresh yeast. Now, that is nowhere near as convenient as using dried yeast unless you happen to live near a bakery who will sell you the fresh yeast. I now use "easy-bake" or "fast-action" dried yeast, which you add straight to the flour, saving time in the preparation.

This recipe makes 2 good-sized naan.

ingredients

35g butter (20ml goes in the
    dough; the rest is to brush
    over the naan)

175g plain white flour (use
    pastry-making flour not strong
    bread flour)
⅔ of a 5ml spoon easy-bake
    dried yeast
⅔ of a 5ml spoon sugar
salt (use plenty)
30ml beaten egg
30ml Greek-style full fat yoghurt
50ml semi-skimmed (2% fat)
    milk at room temperature

[optional] kalonji seeds to
    sprinkle over the naan

vegetable oil to season the pan

kitchen equipment

cast-iron griddle with a diameter
    of 26cm
pastry brush

Put 35g butter into a bowl. Melt the butter by heating it gently in a microwave or by placing the bowl over a pan of boiling water. N.B. just melt the butter; do not heat it so much that it separates into oil and solids.

Sift the flour into a large mixing bowl, add the easy-bake dried yeast, sugar and salt and stir to mix. Pour 20ml melted butter over the flour so you get a long, thin trail of melted butter. Use a fork to work the oil into the flour. Mash up any lumps that form until you get a texture like breadcrumbs. Add the beaten egg and repeat the mixing process.

Spoon the yoghurt over the flour and pour the milk over it. Use the fork to mix in as much of the milk and yoghurt as possible. Now use your hands to bring the dough together and mix it thoroughly. You may need to add a little extra milk to get a smooth dough but only add 5ml at a time and work it into the dough. If you add too much milk the dough will become sticky and will be difficult to knead.

Remove the dough from the bowl. Lightly sprinkle flour on a large chopping board or a clean work surface and start kneading the dough. For tips on kneading bread dough see Cooking Notes.

Knead the dough for 8 minutes allowing it (and you) to rest occasionally. Do not skip this stage or cut short the kneading. If the dough is not kneaded properly it will be difficult to roll out and the bread will have a solid texture.

Put the dough back into the bowl and cover the bowl with cling film. Place the bowl in a warm place (but not in direct heat) for the dough to rise. Depending on the temperature this will take from 1 to 2 hours.

The dough is ready when it has doubled in bulk. Remove the dough from the bowl and cut it in half.

Lightly sprinkle flour on your chopping board or work surface. Take one of the pieces of dough and form it into a circle about 20cm in diameter using a floured rolling pin. Keep rotating the naan as you roll it out. If it starts to stick, sprinkle a little more flour over the board.

If you are using kalonji seeds, sprinkle them thinly over the dough and roll them into the top layer of dough with the rolling pin.

Transfer the prepared naan to a lightly floured plate. Make the other naan in the same way.

Gently re-melt the butter if it has solidified.

Take the cast-iron griddle and heat it on a medium-high heat until it is hot right through.

Use a wad of kitchen paper (thick enough so you won't get your fingers anywhere near the **hot** griddle) and coat the underside with oil. Now spread a coating of oil over the surface of the griddle with the oiled kitchen paper. You should end up with a visible layer of oil on the griddle with little puddles of oil here and there.

Wait for the oil to start lightly smoking before you start cooking the naan.

Slide the first naan off its plate and onto the griddle. While it is cooking, brush the top generously with melted butter using a pastry brush. Some of the kalonji seeds may get dislodged but you can't help that. As the naan cooks, bubbles will appear in the top but don't press them down at this stage.

Cook the first side for about 90 seconds until brown patches start to appear.

Flip the naan over and, this time, press it down onto the griddle with a spatula 2 or 3 times while it is cooking.

Cook the second side for about 60 seconds until it too has brown patches all over.

If an area still has the colour of raw dough press down the uncooked patch onto the griddle with the spatula.

Flip the naan back over and cook for 15 seconds while you brush the top (which will be the side with the kalonji seeds on) with a thin layer of melted butter

Transfer the cooked naan to a serving plate and serve immediately or transfer it to a baking tray to keep warm in the oven while you cook the second naan.

Take lots of crumpled kitchen paper and, taking care to keep your fingers away from the hot griddle, clean the griddle by wiping away any burnt butter and kalonji seeds.

Now repeat the whole process for the second naan.

Paratha

The paratha is my favourite bread served by Indian restaurants. So it's especially disappointing when, at some restaurants, the parathas arrive and they are too oily, too thick and way too stodgy. Perfect parathas should be thin, buttery and flaky.

Traditionally, parathas are cooked on a gently curved metal griddle called a *tava* but a flat cast-iron griddle does the job just as well. If you need help with kneading the dough see Cooking Notes.

This recipe makes 2 lovely parathas.

ingredients

50g butter
175g plain white flour (regular pastry flour not strong bread flour)
salt
½ a 2.5ml spoon sugar
2.5ml baking powder
100ml water
2.5ml white wine vinegar

vegetable oil to season the griddle

kitchen equipment

cast-iron griddle with a diameter of 26cm
pastry brush

Place the butter in a bowl. Melt the butter by heating it gently in a microwave or by placing the bowl over a pan of boiling water. N.B. just melt the butter; do not heat it so much that it separates into oil and solids.

Sift the flour into a large mixing bowl. Add the salt, sugar and baking powder and stir to mix. Pour 20ml of the melted butter over the flour so you get a long, thin trail of melted butter. Use a metal fork to work the butter into the flour. Mash up any lumps that form until you get a texture like breadcrumbs.

Mix the vinegar with 100ml water and pour it over the flour. Use the fork to mix in the water as much as possible. Now use your hands to bring the dough together and mix it thoroughly. If you need a little more water to get a smooth dough, add just 5ml at a time and work it into the dough. If you add too much water the dough will become sticky and will be difficult to knead.

Remove the dough from the bowl. Lightly sprinkle flour onto a large chopping board or a clean work surface and start kneading the dough. For tips on kneading bread dough see Cooking Notes.

Knead the dough for 8 minutes allowing it (and you) to rest occasionally. Do not skip this stage or cut short the kneading. If the dough is not kneaded properly it will be difficult to roll out and the bread will have a solid texture.

Cut the dough in half and put the two halves back into the bowl. Cover the bowl with cling film and leave to rest for at least 1 hour in a warm place. You can make the dough hours in advance if it's more convenient.

Lightly sprinkle flour on your chopping board or work surface. Take one half of the dough and roll it out with a floured rolling pin until you get a thin circle of dough about 22cm in diameter. Keep rotating the dough as you roll it out. If it starts to stick, sprinkle a little more flour on the board.

Now for the fun bit.

Gently re-melt the butter if it has gone solid.

Take a pastry brush and spread a layer of melted butter over the whole surface of the rolled out dough. Now make a cut in the circle of dough from the centre out to the edge.

Start from one side of the cut and roll the dough like the hands of a clock going round until you end up with a cone.

Dust your board with flour. Place the cone with the wide end on the board and then squash the point of the cone down with the palm of your hand to make a ball of dough.

Roll out the ball of dough into a 20cm circle. If butter squishes out just use a little flour to mop it up and incorporate the buttery flour back into the dough.

Slide the paratha onto a lightly floured plate. Make the second paratha in exactly the same way as the first.

Take the cast-iron griddle and spread a thin coating of groundnut oil over the surface with a piece of kitchen paper. Heat the griddle on a medium heat so it is hot right through.

Take one of the parathas and spread a layer of melted butter over the side facing you with a pastry brush. Now flip it over onto the hot griddle so the buttered side is facing the griddle. While it is cooking, butter the side now facing you. Bubbles will appear in the top of the paratha but there's no need to press them down.

Use a spatula to lift up the paratha a little and check the underside. Once you can see brown patches start to appear flip the paratha over and cook the other side.

Flip the paratha over a couple of times to make sure the dough is completely cooked on both sides and that the surfaces have attractive brown patches and a flaky texture. If an area still has the colour of raw dough press down the uncooked patch onto the griddle with the spatula.

Serve immediately or wrap the paratha in kitchen foil and keep it warm in the oven while you cook the second one.

Now repeat the whole process for the second paratha.

Chapati

This recipe makes a rich chapati containing butter and uses chapati flour mixed with plain flour for a lighter bread.

Curiously, the inspiration for this recipe came from Sainsbury's (a UK supermarket). I regularly buy their fresh chapatis which I like to heat in a frying pan with a little oil and eat with my curries in place of rice.

Don't overcook the chapatis or they will end up hard and tough. You want to end up with soft chewy bread and not crisp and flaky like a paratha.

This recipe makes 3 chapatis.

ingredients

15ml melted butter

100g atta (medium-grade chapati flour)

75g plain white flour (regular pastry flour not strong bread flour)

salt

2.5ml baking powder

20ml Greek-style full fat yoghurt

80ml water

2.5ml vinegar

vegetable oil

kitchen equipment

cast-iron griddle with a diameter of 26cm

pastry brush

Place some butter in a bowl (you will need 15ml once it has melted). Melt the butter by gently heating it in a microwave or by placing the bowl over a pan of boiling water. N.B. just melt the butter; do not heat it so much that it separates into oil and solids.

Sift the two types of flour into a large mixing bowl, add the salt and baking powder and stir to mix. Pour 15ml melted butter over the flour so you get a long, thin trail of melted butter. Use a fork to work the butter into the flour. Mash up any lumps that form until you get a texture like breadcrumbs.

Spoon the yoghurt onto the flour. Mix the vinegar with 80ml water and pour it over the flour. Use the fork to mix in the water and yoghurt as far as possible. Now use your hands to bring the dough together and mix it thoroughly. If you need a little more water to get a smooth dough, add just 5ml at a time and work it into the dough. If you add too much water the dough will become sticky and will be difficult to knead.

Remove the dough from the bowl. Lightly flour a large chopping board or a clean work surface and start kneading the dough. For tips on kneading bread dough see Cooking Notes.

Knead the dough for 8 minutes allowing it (and you) to rest occasionally. Do not skip this stage or cut short the kneading. If the dough is not kneaded properly it will be difficult to roll out and the bread will have a solid texture.

Cut the dough into 3 equal pieces and put them back into the bowl. Cover the bowl with cling film and leave to rest for at least 1 hour in a warm place. You can make the dough hours in advance if it's more convenient.

Lightly sprinkle flour onto your chopping board or work surface. Take one piece of the dough and roll it out with a floured rolling pin until you get a thin circle of dough about 20cm in diameter. Keep rotating the dough as you roll it out. If it starts to stick, sprinkle a little more flour on the board.

Slide the chapati onto a lightly floured plate. Make the other 2 chapatis in exactly the same way.

Take the cast-iron griddle and heat it on a medium-high heat until it is hot right through.

Use a wad of kitchen paper (thick enough so you won't get your fingers anywhere near the hot griddle) and coat the underside with oil. Now spread a coating of oil over the surface with the oiled kitchen paper. You should end up with a visible layer of oil on the griddle with little puddles of oil here and there.

Wait for the oil to start lightly smoking before you start cooking the chapatis.

Slide one of the chapatis onto the griddle. While it is cooking, brush the top lightly with vegetable oil using a pastry brush. As the chapati cooks, bubbles will appear in the top but don't press them down at this stage.

Cook the first side for about 90 seconds until brown patches start to appear.

Flip the chapati over and, this time, press it down onto the griddle with a spatula 2 or 3 times while it is cooking.

Cook the second side for about 60 seconds until it looks just like the first side

If an area still has the colour of raw dough press down the uncooked patch onto the griddle with the spatula.

Serve immediately or wrap the chapati in kitchen foil and keep it warm in the oven while you cook the other ones.

Now repeat the whole process for the other 2 chapatis.

Dips and Relishes

A restaurant-style meal is not complete without some spicy dips and relishes.

When you order poppadoms in a restaurant you will invariably get offered the relish tray to liven them up. A typical relish tray might have some mango chutney, a fresh onion relish, lime pickle and a minty yoghurt dip.

We are not going to go to the bother of making our own mango chutney or lime pickle, so you need to buy them from the supermarket or your nearest Asian grocers. This chapter does include my recipes for the fresh onion relish and the minty yoghurt dip. In addition, there are recipes for a tamarind dip and a fresh tomato relish. Tamarind Dip is sweet and sour and strongly flavoured. Tomato Relish is an Asian version of salsa and is fresh and spicy.

All four of the dips and relishes use ground, dry-roasted cumin seeds. If you're making a selection of dips and relishes it's a good idea to dry roast and grind sufficient cumin seeds to make all the recipes.

The dips and relishes are also ideal served with onion bhajis and some shredded lettuce as a simple starter.

Yoghurt Dip

This is the minty yoghurt dip you get with poppadoms and onion bhajis in a restaurant. The recipe is pretty much the same as the one in The Curry House Cookery Book. I have tried altering the recipe a few times but I always come back to this one as it's easily my favourite.

The dip tends to come out thicker than its restaurant counterpart but that means you can get plenty of dip on your poppadom without it dripping off.

Using yellow food colouring is entirely optional. The colouring does nothing for the taste of the dip but it does make it look pretty. Without the colouring the dip comes out a pale beige colour. Don't be tempted to use turmeric as a substitute for the artificial yellow colouring. Although it is a natural colouring, it will add the wrong taste to the dip.

ingredients

175ml Greek-style full fat
   yoghurt
2.5ml English mint sauce
   (preferably Colman's)
2.5ml sugar
½ a 2.5ml spoon ground dry-
   roasted cumin seeds
½ a 2.5ml spoon amchoor
   powder
2 pinches *hot* chilli powder
3 pinches garlic powder
2 grinds black peppercorns
salt
water
[optional] yellow food colouring
   powder

Put all the ingredients except the water and food colouring into a bowl and beat with a whisk.

[optional] Carefully add the yellow food colouring powder to the yoghurt. Use literally just the very tip of a spoon at a time. Mix each tiny amount of colouring thoroughly into the yoghurt before you add more. You are trying to achieve the colour of pale egg yolk.

Add a little water, whisk and repeat the process until you get the desired consistency. I prefer mine a bit thicker than the restaurant version but it should still be runny enough to pour from a spoon.

Leave the dip to mature for about 30 minutes (preferably longer). Stir once or twice during this time to re-mix the ingredients.

If you are making the dip some time in advance then refrigerate it as soon as it's made. Bring the dip back to room temperature before using.

Tamarind Dip

If you love the combination of hot, sweet and sour flavours then this is the dip for you.

Some restaurants offer a tamarind dip with their poppadoms but this is my version of the dip you get from Ambala, which is a chain of shops selling Indian and Pakistani snacks and sweets. There is an Ambala store close to the shop where I buy my spices and I always seem to pop in to bring myself home a spicy lunch of samosas and pakoras accompanied by their tamarind dip.

I have no idea exactly what goes into Ambala's version but this is my recipe for a hot, sweet and sour tamarind dip.

ingredients

30ml tamarind paste

1 fat spring onion – finely chopped (use 2 if they are very thin)

5ml sugar

¼ of a 2.5ml spoon ground dry-roasted cumin seeds

1 pinch **hot** chilli powder (more if you like it quite hot)

[optional] salt – the tamarind paste will probably be salty enough

water – about 10ml but it will depend on how thick your tamarind paste is

Remove the root from the spring onion and thinly slice the white part, discarding the green part. Now chop the onion slices as finely as possible.

Put all the ingredients except the water into a bowl and beat with a small whisk.

Add a little water, whisk and repeat the process until you get the desired consistency. The dip should be quite runny but don't dilute the taste too much. Keep tasting before you add more water.

Leave the dip to mature for about 30 minutes (preferably longer). Stir once or twice during this time to re-mix the ingredients.

If you are making the dip some time in advance then refrigerate it as soon as it's made. Bring the dip back to room temperature before using.

Onion Relish

You can buy "sweet" onions from the supermarket these days and they are ideal for making Onion Relish. Sweet onions are less harsh than regular onions when eaten raw, although they never appear to be particularly sweet to me.

You should really make this relish as far in advance as possible so the flavours blend together nicely. But, if you have to make it at the last minute, it's still pretty good.

ingredients

1 sweet onion (about 100g trimmed weight)
1 good-sized tomato
10ml finely chopped coriander leaves
3 pinches ground dry-roasted cumin seeds
salt

Trim, peel and finely chop the sweet onion.

Slide the tomato into a bowl of boiling water and leave for 2 minutes. Remove the tomato and plunge it into cold water. Dry the tomato, slice it into quarters and peel off the skin. Remove the seeds and pith and then chop the tomato flesh into small chunks.

Place the finely chopped onion, chopped tomato and all the other ingredients in a bowl and stir to mix the ingredients.

Leave the relish to mature for about 30 minutes (preferably longer). Stir once or twice during this time to re-mix the ingredients.

If you are making the relish some time in advance then refrigerate it as soon as it's made. Bring the relish back to room temperature before using.

Tomato Relish

I suppose you could think of Tomato Relish as a kind of Asian salsa. It is delicious with any of the tandoori-style and kebab dishes. It is also ideal as one of a selection of relishes, dips and chutneys which you serve with poppadoms or onion bhajis.

Try to make sure your tomatoes are perfectly ripe. If not, you may have to increase the amount of sugar a little to make sure the sweet/sour balance of the relish is maintained.

ingredients

3 good-sized, ripe tomatoes

1 fat spring onion – finely chopped (use 2 if they are very thin)

1 long, thin green chilli – finely chopped

7.5ml tamarind paste

10ml finely chopped coriander leaves

½ a 2.5ml spoon ground dry-roasted cumin seeds

[optional] a little sugar

salt (be careful, the tamarind paste will contain salt)

Slide the tomatoes into a bowl of boiling water and leave for 2 minutes. Remove the tomatoes and plunge them into cold water. Dry the tomatoes, slice each into quarters and peel off the skin. Remove the seeds and pith and then chop the tomato flesh into small chunks. Set aside.

Remove the root from the spring onion and thinly slice the white part, discarding the green part. Now finely chop the onion slices.

Top and tail the chilli, slice in half lengthways and remove the seeds and pith by running a teaspoon along the length of the chilli halves. Finely chop the chilli flesh.

Put the chopped tomato, chopped spring onion, chopped chilli and all the other ingredients into a bowl and stir to mix.

Leave the relish to mature for about 30 minutes (preferably longer). Stir once or twice during this time to re-mix the ingredients.

If you are making the relish some time in advance then refrigerate it as soon as it's made. Bring the relish back to room temperature before using.

Alternatives to Chicken

All of the recipes for the Curry House Favourites and many of the House Specials are made using chicken as the main ingredient but it's very easy to convert any of those recipes so they feature lamb, king prawns or a vegetarian option instead.

Restaurants use the same sauce for, say, Chicken Madras as for Lamb Madras and there's no reason why we can't do the same. All you need to do is change the main ingredient and alter the method a little.

The following pages give you detailed instructions on how to amend the recipes to use the main ingredient of your choice.

Lamb

I did a lot of testing to find the best way to cook lamb for these recipes. I tried grilling the lamb leg steaks and I tried cooking them in the oven but the best method by far was to cut the steaks into strips and stir fry them over a high heat.

The benefits of this method are that it gives the lamb an excellent flavour, the lamb comes out very tender and it cooks very quickly. Stir frying the strips of lamb over a high heat sears the meat so it turns brown. However, browning the lamb does create one side effect, which is that it darkens the final colour of the curry a little. Personally, I don't find this a problem and the benefits far outweigh the one disadvantage.

Amend the ingredients, kitchen equipment and the method as follows:

omit	*insert*
ingredients	
• 350g chicken breast	• 400g prime lamb leg steaks (to give 300g lean meat when trimmed)
kitchen equipment	
• *nil*	• large karahi or wok
method	
• While the onion mixture is cooking, skin the chicken breasts, remove any connective tissue and cut the meat into chunks about 25mm square.	• While the onion mixture is cooking, trim the lamb. Lamb leg steaks are structured like a cartwheel, so separate the meat along the "spokes" of connective tissue. Now trim off all the tissue and the fat from the edge of the steaks. Slice the remaining fillets of lean meat into strips about 40mm long and 12mm wide. Some

awkward-shaped bits will be smaller but that's OK.

- Raise the heat to medium and add the chicken chunks. Stir until the pieces of chicken have turned white over most of their surface.

- Add a little oil to the karahi and wipe with kitchen paper so the whole surface of the karahi is covered with a thin layer of oil. Heat the karahi over a high heat.

- Simmer the chicken for 15 minutes (less if you used small chunks).

- Simmer the sauce for 15 minutes.

- While the sauce is cooking, divide the strips of lamb into 2 batches. Take the first batch of lamb and slide the strips into the hot karahi. Stir fry on a high heat for about 2 minutes, then reduce the heat to medium and cook the lamb until it is no longer pink in the middle (about another 1-2 minutes). Transfer the lamb onto a large cold plate to rest. Add a few drops of oil to the karahi and repeat the process for the second batch of lamb.

- *nil*

- 3 minutes before the end of the cooking add the fried strips of lamb to the sauce and stir to mix. Discard the juice that has gathered on the plate. Bring back the sauce to a gentle simmer to re-heat the lamb. Make sure the lamb is piping hot before you serve the dish.

Prawns

The recipe for King Prawn Sizzler in the House Specials chapter calls for raw prawns. The recipe uses a karahi from start to finish so it's convenient to cook the prawns from raw and it does give the very best flavour. However, to make a prawn version of one of the chicken recipes it's much easier to use ready-cooked king prawns. If your king prawns are frozen make sure they are thoroughly defrosted before you add them to the curry.

Amend the ingredients and the method as follows:

omit	*insert*
ingredients	
• 350g chicken breast	• 225g cooked king prawns – thawed if previously frozen
method	
• While the onion mixture is cooking, skin the chicken breasts, remove any connective tissue and cut the meat into chunks about 25mm square.	• While the onion mixture is cooking, take the king prawns out of the fridge and spread them out on a plate so they are not too cold when you need to heat them through.
• Raise the heat to medium and add the chicken chunks. Stir until the pieces of chicken have turned white over most of their surface.	• Dry the prawns with kitchen paper so they do not add too much liquid to the sauce near the end of the cooking.
• Simmer the chicken for 15 minutes (less if you used small chunks)	• Simmer the sauce for 15 minutes
• *nil*	• 3 minutes before the end of the cooking add the king prawns to the sauce and stir

to mix. Bring the sauce to barely a simmer and heat through the prawns. Do not boil the sauce or the prawns will end up unpleasantly chewy. Make sure the prawns are piping hot before you serve the dish.

Vegetarian

If you want to make a vegetarian version of any of the chicken curries you have three main alternatives:

1. A meat substitute like soya chunks or Quorn. Quorn is ready-cooked and only needs heating through. Add Quorn to your curry at the same point as you would add the chicken. Use about 240g Quorn. Textured soya chunks need re-hydrating and then cooking, so follow the instructions on the packet and adapt the recipe accordingly.

2. The larger beans such as red kidney beans or, my favourite, black eye beans. To save time and effort use tinned beans which are already re-hydrated and cooked. Drain any liquid from the beans and add them to the curry at the same time as you would the chicken. Stir gently from time to time, being careful not to mash up the beans. Use a 410g tin, which will give you about 240g of beans when drained.

3. Vegetables can be used in much the same way as in the recipe for Aloo Gobi. The choice of vegetables is yours but, for potatoes and cauliflower, amend the ingredients and the method as follows:

omit	*insert*
ingredients	
• 350g chicken breast	• 200g boiling potatoes (trimmed weight)
	• 200g cauliflower (trimmed weight)
method	
• While the onion mixture is cooking, skin the chicken breasts, remove any connective tissue and cut the meat into chunks about 25mm square.	• While the onion mixture is cooking, take a large saucepan, fill it ¾ full of water and get the water boiling.
	• Wash and peel the potatoes and weigh

out the required 200g. Slice the potatoes into rounds about 18mm thick. Chop each round into rough cubes.

- Wash the cauliflower and weigh out the required 200g. Cut the cauliflower into florets about 25mm across at the widest part.
- When the water comes to a boil, carefully lower the potato cubes and cauliflower florets into the water. Return the water to the boil and simmer the vegetables for 10 minutes. Drain the vegetables into a sieve and then gently tip them out onto a large plate to dry off a little.

- Raise the heat to medium and add the chicken chunks. Stir until the pieces of chicken have turned white over most of their surface.

- *nil*

- Simmer the chicken for 15 minutes (less if you used small chunks).

- Simmer the sauce for 15 minutes.

- *nil*

- 5 minutes before the end of the cooking add the cooked vegetables to the sauce and stir in very gently with a metal tablespoon. Don't use a thick wooden or plastic spoon or you risk breaking up the vegetables as you stir them. Make sure the vegetables are completely coated in sauce and bring the sauce back to a gentle simmer. Gently stir the vegetables a couple of times as they finish cooking.

Substitute Ingredients

There may be some times where you can't get hold of one or more of the ingredients in a recipe. Using an alternative ingredient will change the taste or texture of the dish but it's still better than not making the dish at all.

Here is a list of suggestions for substitutes:

ingredient	substitute	how to use
amchoor (green mango powder)	fresh lime juice + sugar	If you cannot get amchoor use the same volume of fresh lime juice plus a pinch of sugar. For marinades, reduce other liquids by a corresponding amount.
black cardamom pod	green cardamom pod	Use 2 green cardamom pods for every 1 black cardamom pod. Green cardamoms do not have the same robust and almost smoky flavour but are a decent substitute.
black cumin seed	regular cumin seed	Directly substitute regular cumin seed

cassia bark	cinnamon quills	Use half the size of true cinnamon in place of cassia bark
	ground cinnamon	Use 1.25ml in place of a piece of cassia bark about 8mm by 30mm
creamed coconut	coconut powder	Use 15ml for every 15ml spoon of chopped creamed coconut.
English mint sauce	fresh mint + vinegar + sugar	For each 5ml of mint sauce use 5ml of finely chopped mint, 2.5ml malt vinegar and 1.25ml sugar.
fenugreek, dried leaves (*kasuri methi*)	*no substitute*	Fenugreek seeds are not a good substitute – think of the difference in taste between coriander seeds and fresh coriander leaves (cilantro). The best idea is to buy a few packs with a long life either in a shop or by mail order. Fenugreek leaves are very strong tasting so you only need a small amount. Once you open the pack you should store the remainder in a sealed jar or the leaves will give your kitchen a permanent curry house smell.
ginger, fresh grated	ground dried ginger	Use grated fresh ginger whenever possible but, if you

can't get hold of fresh ginger, then ground dried ginger is a passable alternative. Use half the volume of ground dried ginger as grated fresh ginger.

paprika, smoked	regular paprika + chilli powder	If you can't get hold of smoked paprika use a mixture of ⅔ regular paprika plus ⅓ hot chilli powder.
tamarind paste	tamarind concentrate	Tamarind concentrate is dark brown with a thick and sticky consistency like treacle, whereas tamarind paste has a consistency similar to tomato ketchup. Use ⅓ the amount of tamarind concentrate as tamarind paste.
yoghurt, Greek-style full fat	*no substitute*	Low fat yoghurt is likely to split into solids and liquids when heated so cannot be used as a substitute.

Notes for American Readers

It is clear from chatting to American friends on internet food groups that we do not always use the same terms for the same ingredients or the same piece of kitchen equipment. So I have created a small glossary which converts British English cooking terms into their American equivalents. I hope my American readers will find it useful and a good way to avoid any confusion.

The recipes use metric weights and measures. American readers will be accustomed to weights being expressed in ounces and volume measurements in cups, so I have constructed a table which gives conversions from metric to American units for the common weights and measures used in the book. Some of the conversions are, by necessity, rounded but the table gives you a fair idea of what you need for a particular recipe. The table also includes conversions from millimetres to inches and for oven temperatures.

Ingredients and Cooking Terms

British English	American English
aubergine	eggplant
barbecue (noun and verb)	grill
chapati flour (medium *atta*)	wheat flour with a fiber content of about 5%
chilli powder	pure ground red chili peppers **N.B.** *not the chili powder used for making chili which contains added ingredients*
chillies, thin green	green Cayenne chili peppers
cling film	plastic wrap
cookery book	cookbook
coriander leaf	cilantro
courgette	zucchini
cream:	
double cream	heavy cream
single cream	light cream
desiccated coconut	shredded coconut
English mint sauce	chopped mint preserved in malt vinegar and sugar
flaked almonds	slivered almonds
frying pan	skillet
Greek-style full fat yoghurt	yogurt made with full cream milk *do not substitute low fat yogurt – it will split*

grill (noun and verb)	broil
karahi	a bowl-shaped cooking pan like a Chinese wok but with two handles instead of one - use a large wok as a substitute
king prawn (jumbo)	large shrimp (about ½ inch-⅝inch diameter when raw)
kitchen foil	aluminum foil
kitchen paper	paper towel
minced lamb	ground lamb
pepper, red / green	bell pepper
plain flour	all-purpose flour
prawn	shrimp
scales (kitchen)	scale
spring onion	scallion
starters	appetizers
sweet pepper	bell pepper
tin (as in tinned coconut milk)	can
wholemeal flour	whole wheat flour with a fiber content of about 9%

Conversion table for weights and measures

Metric volumes	American equivalent (rounded)
2.5ml	½ teaspoon
5ml	1 teaspoon
10ml	2 teaspoons
15ml	1 tablespoon
20ml	4 teaspoons
30ml	2 tablespoons
45ml	3 tablespoons
60ml	¼ cup / 4 tablespoons
80ml	⅜ cup
120ml	½ cup
175ml	¾ cup
237ml	1 cup
400ml	1¾ cups

Metric weights	American equivalent (rounded)
28g	1 ounce
50g	1¾ ounces
75g	2⅝ ounces
100g	3½ ounces
125g	4⅜ ounces
150g	5¼ ounces
175g	6¼ ounces
200g	7 ounces
225g	8 ounces
250g	8⅞ ounces
300g	10½ ounces
350g	12⅜ ounces
375g	13¼ ounces
400g	14 ounces
475g	16¾ ounces

Metric measurements	American equivalent (rounded)
3mm	⅛ inch
6mm	¼ inch
10mm	⅜ inch
12mm	½ inch
20mm	¾ inch
25mm	1 inch
30mm	1⅛ inches
35mm	1⅜ inches
40mm	1⅝ inches
70mm = 7cm	2¾ inches
20cm	7⅞ inches
22cm	8⅝ inches
26cm	10¼ inches
30.5cm	12 inches

Oven temperatures	American equivalent
Gas 6 / 200°C	400°F
Gas 7 / 220°C	425°F

Online Pictures of the Recipes

The cost of full-colour printing would have made this book prohibitively expensive, so it was not possible to include photos of the finished recipes other than the excellent cover photos taken by Graham Alder of MMStudios in Oxford.

However, there are pictures of every recipe from this book available for you to look at online. The photos are an accurate record of how each recipe in the book turned out for me.

The dishes have not been professionally arranged for the photos by a "food stylist" like magazine photos and coffee table cookery books. Instead, the pictures show what you can confidently expect the dishes to look like when you've made them. Take the kofta recipe for example - most books would picture the sauce with the fried meatballs resting prettily on top. But in the recipe you need to cook the meatballs in the sauce for five minutes for the flavours to cross over from meatball to sauce and vice versa. So the photo shows you the meatballs covered in sauce, exactly how you would serve the dish yourself.

If you would like to view the pictures please visit:

www.curryhouse.co.uk/bonus

Index

A
Achar 40
almonds, flaked 92
almonds, ground 59, 87, 92
Aloo Gobi 157
American cooking terms
  196
American measures 198
aubergine 150
B
baking tray 27
Balti 49
Bhindi Bhaji 145
Bhuna 84
Bombay Aloo 140
bread
    chapati 174
    naan 167
    paratha 171
Brinjal Bhaji 150
Butter Chicken 46
C
cardamom, ground 17
cashew nut purée 34, 101
casserole pan 25
cassia bark 17
cauliflower 143, 157
Cauliflower Bhaji 143

Chapati 174
chicken
    curries - most of the
    recipes for curries in
    House Specials and all
    Curry House Favourites
    use chicken 10
    general 17
    mini-fillets 18
    using lamb, prawns or a
    vegetarian option instead
    of chicken 183
Chicken Shashlik Bhuna 63
chicken tikka
    Chicken Tikka 119
    Chicken Tikka Masala
    101
    Herb Chicken Tikka 123
    Tamarind Chicken Tikka
    121
Chicken with Coconut 66
Chicken with Tomatoes and
  Coriander 55
chilli powder 18
chillies, dried red 114
chillies, fresh green 37, 58,
  98
coconut

cream 87
milk 66
uses 19
coriander leaves   19
cream 47, 88, 93
cumin seeds, dry-roasted 20
D
dhal 107, 147
Dhansak 107
Dopiaza 95
dry roasting 14
E
English mint sauce 20
F
food blender 27
food grater 25
G
garam masala 20
garlic 21
Garlic Chicken 52
ghee 15, 21
ginger 21
griddle 27
grinds 15
H
Herb Chicken Tikka 123
J
Jalfrezi 98

Jeera Murgh 43

K

karahi 26

Karahi King Prawns 130

King Prawn Sizzler 72

kitchen scales 26

kneading dough 15

knife, chopping herbs 26

Korma 87

L

Lamb Chops with Ginger
    128

lamb curries 184

Lamb Koftas 75

lemon

    juice 21

    slices 59

    wild 58

lentils 107, 147

lime

    juice 21

    pickle 40, 177

    slices 41

M

Madras 89

mashing the onions, garlic
    and ginger 13

measuring spoons 14, 26

meatballs 75

mint

    ingredient 41, 61, 128,
        178

    leaves 21

sauce 20

mortar and pestle 26

Mushroom Bhaji 153

N

Naan 167

O

okra 145

onion 22

Onion Bhajis 137

Onion Relish 180

P

palak 155

Paratha 171

Pasanda 92

Patia 111

pestle and mortar 26

pictures of the recipes 201

Pilau Rice 163

pinch 14

Plain Rice 166

portions 13

potato 140, 157

potato masher 25

prawn curries 186

prawns 72, 130

Pudina Murgh 61

R

Rezala 37

rice

    pilau 163

    plain 166

    re-heating 16

Rogan Josh 81

S

Saag (curry) 104

Saag Bhaji 155

salt 22

Satkara 58

Seekh Kebabs 133

Shahi Chicken 34

simmering 13

spinach 104, 155

substitute ingredients 191

Subzi Murgh 69

T

Tamarind Chicken 31

Tamarind Chicken Tikka 121

Tamarind Dip 179

tamarind paste 22

Tandoori-style Chicken 125

Tarka Dhal 147

Tikka Masala 101

tomato 22

tomato paste 23

Tomato Relish 181

V

vegetable curry 157

vegetarian curries 188

Vindaloo 114

W

water, adding to curries 14

website 201

wire rack 27

Y

yoghurt 23

Yoghurt Dip 178

Made in the USA
San Bernardino, CA
14 December 2014